Informal Sector in A Developing Economy

Informal Sector
in
A Developing Economy

Dr. Utpal Chowdhury

ANMOL PUBLICATIONS PVT. LTD.
NEW DELHI - 110 002 (INDIA)

ANMOL PUBLICATIONS PVT. LTD.
H.O.: 4374/4B, Ansari Road, Daryaganj
New Delhi - 110 002
Ph.: 23261597, 23278000
B.O.: No. 1015, Ist Main Road, BSK III Stage
III Phase, III Block
Bangalore - 560 085 (India)
Visit us at: www.anmolpublications.com

Informal Sector in A Developing Economy

First Published, 2006

ISBN 81-261-2638-8

PRINTED IN INDIA

Published by J.L. Kumar for Anmol Publications Pvt. Ltd., New Delhi - 110 002 and Printed at Mehra Offset Press, Delhi.

Contents

	Preface	*vii*
	List of Tables	*ix*
	Abbreviations	*xi*
1.	Introduction: Conceptual Framework of the Informal Sector	1
2.	A Close Look at Some of the Major Informal Industries in Calcutta	24
3.	Highlighting Informal Slum Industries Around Calcutta	59
4.	The Organisation of Work in the Informal Sector	85
5.	Barriers to Development of the Informal Sector and Some Related Issues	118
6.	Employment Potential of the Informal Sector	148
7.	Suggestions for an Upliftment of the Garbage Pickers	174
8.	Strategies for an All Round Development of the Informal Sector	188
9.	Informal Sector in the Indian Context	206
	Bibliography	221
	Index	225

Preface

Employment, globally, is a much talked about issue. So long we have been experienced with different so called 'employment growth' models. Frankly, not much has come out of it. The gap between the employment opportunity and the number of growing labour force still presents a dreadful picture.

The problem of unemployment gets worse now owing to the overlapping impact of globalization, liberalization, open market economy and the likes. Even the security of the 'organized sectors' jobs are now becoming called in question.

Observing this frontier view, we have considered it prudent enough to search for mass employment opportunity beneath the stair. And finally, we find it in the 'Informal Sector'—a mass labour absorber throughout the globe.

This book delves deep into the study of the 'Informal Sector' from all possible angles. To this end, I am highly indebted to my revered Professor, Dr. Shaktipada Mukherjee of the Department of Commerce, University of Calcutta who contributed invaluable guidance in completing this work. I must be grateful to my learned colleagues along with my wife Mrs. Anurupa Chowdhury and my beloved daughter Shyama Priya Chowdhury whose wholehearted co-operation in this regard was beyond my expectation.

Kolkata *Utpal Chowdhury*

List of Tables

1.1:	Usage of Criteria Relating to Informal Sector	12-13
1.2:	Some Useful Information about the Small Tanners	39
1.3:	Distribution of Units by Capital Structure	42
1.4:	Structure of Ownership	43
1.5:	Weighted Average Wage	46
1.6:	Source wise Distribution of Borrowed Capital	47
1.7:	Distribution of Clay Modellers by Age Group	50
1.8:	Classification of Clay Modellers	50
1.9:	Distribution of the Units by Industrial Group	64
1.10:	Age of Surveyed Units	64
1.11:	Workshop Area of the Surveyed Units	66
1.12:	Distribution of Employment of Surveyed Units	67
1.13:	Distribution of Surveyed Workers by Size of Weekly Wages	68
1.14:	Distribution of Surveyed Units by Capital and Employment Size	71
1.15:	Distribution of Surveyed Units by Capital and Turnover Size	72
1.16:	Distribution of Surveyed Units by Capital and Value Added Size	73
1.17:	Duration of Credit Given by Surveyed Units to Their Buyers	75

1.18:	Main Constraints Reported by Unit-Owners	75
1.19:	A Tit Bit about the Recuperative Work	95-96
1.20:	Socio-Economic Features of the Garbage Packers of Bantala Dumping Ground, Calcutta	100
1.21:	Selected Economies in the ESCAP Region	141
1.22:	Four Sector Input-Output Model	160
1.23:	The Seasonal Fluctuation in the Price of Waste Material	184

Abbreviations

CITU	:	Centre of Indian Trade Union.
CMC	:	Calcutta Municipal Corporation.
CMDA	:	Calcutta Metropolitan Development Authority.
CMERI	:	Central Mechanical Engineering Research Institute.
DCSSI	:	Directorate of Cottage and Small-Scale Industries.
ESCAP	:	Economic and Social Survey of Asia and The Pacific.
ILO	:	International Labour Organisation.
INTUC	:	Indian National Trade Union Congress.
ISI	:	Indian Standard Institution.
LDC	:	Less Developed Countries.
ORG	:	Operations Research Group.
SISI	:	Small Industries Service Institute.
SSI	:	Small-Scale Industries.
UK	:	United Kingdom.
USA	:	United States of America.
WEP	:	World Employment Programme.

1

Introduction: Conceptual Framework of the Informal Sector*

The term 'Informal Sector' derives its origin from the dualistic concept formally put forth by Lewis (1954) and Fei and Ranis (1964). The rapid diffusion of this term, however, emerges through a much quoted paper presented by Hart (1971) in a conference on urban unemployment in Africa who for the sakė of describing the dichotomous nature of the urban economy of Ghana used this term for the first time. He evaluates the productivity of the informal sector as an employment outlet, which was so long relegated in terms of urban research and policies.

PREAMBLE

For more practical reasons, the concept of informal sector has finally been incorporated in the ILO's World Employment Programme. Consequently, a series of country studies were undertaken which explore the unemployment problem of the developing economics from various aspects. The major contributions of these country missions were

---

* An abstract of the concept of 'Informal Sector' was presented as a seminar paper in the twelfth annual conference, February 1992 of the Bengal Economics Association, Kolkata.

For a critical note of this portion of our work, please see: Chowdhury Dr.U.K. [2000]: "An Alternative Approach To Informal Sector" in *The Asian Economic Review* (Hyderabad, India), December 2000, Vol. 42, No. 3, pp : 470-479.

the identification of several dimensions relating to employment and the evolvement of a new approach towards the urban traditional sector which was ultimately incorporated into the concept of informal sector.

Borrowing the same model of the country studies, the ILO - WEP city studies placed greater emphasis on the productive role of the informal sector in terms of growth and redistribution. The remarkable contribution of the ILO - WEP city studies was that these studies induce a 'target group' approach to policy recommendations and trace out the 'working poor' as a particular category within the urban economy requiring special attention.

However, all characteristics of the informal sector, as laid down by different studies, can be grouped under three categories; those characteristics, which lay down specific emphasis on the enterprise, may form the first category. In the second category, those features can be placed which disclose the nature of exchange relationship between the state and the informal sector and the third category can be formed by those characteristics which are based on the employment situation or labour market processes.

In the conclusion, it can be said that only three basic areas of the informal sector concept have so far been explores. There is enough room for further studies which might be helpful for rectifying the theoretical inadequacies of the formal/ informal dualistic model.

Origin of the Concept

The theoretical basis of the concept 'Informal' sector is deeply rooted in the dichotomy of the urban economy of the third world countries. The models of sectoral dualism were first introduced by Lewis[a] and Fei and Ranis[b]. In their formulations, the modern capitalist sector is the dynamic one and the growth of this sector depends on the expansion of output and on the ploughing back of profit. The exodus of labour from the surplus of the traditional sector to the modern sector is assumed to be unlimited at constant real wages. The extention of the urban traditional sector induces a dichotomous character to the urban economy.

To explain such a dichotomy, the term 'Informal' sector was first used by Hart[c]. In September, 1971, a conference on 'urban unemployment in Africa' was held by the Institute of Development Studies at the University of Sussex. At the conference, Hart presented his much quoted paper on the informal sector, based on his work in the low income neighbourhood of NIMA in ACCRA. During his field work, he traced out a vast self-employed sector which absorbed a countable new entrants to the urban labour force who were unable to obtain employment in the formal sector. He did not agree with the traditional outlook of treating this sector as being highly unproductive. Due to this attitude, numerous diversified activities likely to fall in this sector were neglected so long both in terms of urban research and policies.

In the aforesaid conference, John Weeks[d] presented a paper reviewing the literature on urban unemployment and introducing the concept of the 'unremunerated' sector, - a close intellectual cousin of the 'informal' sector. The discussions held in the conference act as a springboard for the informal sector concept. Within a year, the concept was incorporated in revised form into the ILO report on Kenya[e]. From then on, this particular sector was incorporated into the conceptual underpinnings of a considerable numbers of urban researches in the ILO's World Employment Programme and consequently into the urban research programme of other international organizations. As a result, a whole gamut of research work was directed towards this particular arena and an international academic and policy - prescribing network came into being around the concept and its application.

However, for the purpose of clarifying the concept of informal sector, most of the related studies have commonly adopted a 'two sector' terminology and mode of analysis. In particular, the 'two sector' approach is characterised by the divisions of economic activities and employment into 'traditional' and 'modern' sector, viewing the latter as a result of a number of factors like foreign investment, application of advanced technologies and the advent of sophisticated professional and governmental activities. While the former has been considered as a pre - capitalist mode of production, which survives, even in the face of penetration created by the western capitalism.

The two - sector approach has been boosted up with the presentation of Hart's influential paper on urban employment as mentioned already. The dualistic approach as introduced by Hart was something new in the sense that it divides the economic activities as formal and informal instead of modern and traditional. He emphasized the significance of self - employment and the degree of statistical underestimation in the informal sector. However, his model was based exclusively on a distinction between wage earning and self - employment with the key variable being the extent of relationship of work. The originality of this model lies in the identification of new income generating activities in the informal sector.

The ILO Country Mission

For practical purposes, the concept of informal sector has been aired publicly and the chronic and intractable unemployment in every developing country, due to the failure of the expected trickle down effect under the accelerated growth policy, had finally become the subject of international agency debate. The ILO's employment policy convention (no: 122) committed governments to adopt 'active full employment policies'. An additional step was the implementation of the world employment programme at the ILO, 1969 session. In order to analyse the problems of unemployment as well as to frame out policies accordingly, a series of country studies were undertaken to evolve 'employment oriented strategies of development'.

The ILO country missions played an important role in the development of a new outlook on the employment problem. The prime objective of all these missions was to highlight the consequences of varying types of 'accelerated growth' development strategies in terms of 'structural imbalances'. As the Kenya Mission[f] noted in its preamble: "It is increasingly clear that these employment problems are closely related to inequalities in income and opportunities which are not merely among their consequences but among their causes as well. Thus, social justice and a fair distribution of benefits of growth are not only needed for their own sakes but have become conditions for eradicating unemployment.

The Colombia mission[g] enumerated three distinct but related dimensions of unemployment. These are: lack of employment opportunities, lack of adequate sources of income and a volume of unutilised or under utilised labour[h].

The conclusion of this mission was that "poverty, therefore, emerges as the most compelling aspect of the employment problem in Colombia"[I]. In order to solve unemployment, their recommendations were: structural and institutional changes, ranging from land and fiscal reform and limiting consumption expenditure, to the development of labour - intensive urban industrial employment in such areas construction and handicrafts[j].

The Sri Lanka mission recommended a full employment strategy through such measures as land reforms for absorbing more rural workers and wages policy to reduce differentials and limit consumption growth to a minimum. Besides, it also recommended the reorganisation of the educational system to cope with structural imbalances.

The Kenya mission like the Colombia mission , but with greater clarity, enumerated four basic imbalances : at the global level, the gap between the existing capacity of the economy to provide productive employment opportunities and the large number of job seekers; 'centre - periphery' imbalances due to large scale migration; imbalances in education between the prevailing education system and job opportunities available; and finally , imbalances caused by partial treatment of or lack of support for , the informal as against the formal sector. The Kenya mission has emphasized on the rectification of these structural imbalances and on the productive role of the informal sector. In addition, the mission recommended a speedy promotion of this sector through ceasing of demolition of informal sector housing and intensifying research on products suitable for production or use in the informal sector.

The major contribution of the country mission relating

to employment can be narrated as: [k] first, they contributed to the improvement of a comprehensive approach to employment; second, they helped to define different aspects of the employment; third, they traced out the specific imbalances responsible for creating unemployment problem in the developing countries and finally, they contributed to the evolvement of a new outlook to the so - called 'traditional' urban sector. Through the different reports, a specific progression was made towards this new outlook, which was ultimately incorporated into the concept of informal sector.

The ILO—WEP City Studies

Borrowing the same model of the country studies, the city studies under ILO's World Employment Programme also laid an emphasis on the productive role of the informal sector in terms of growth and redistribution. The city studies did go beyond this generalisation for searching out its local implications. For example, the Calcutta study[l] revealed some structural imbalances in the labour market. Calcutta's problems are, in fact, a reflection of several structural disparities, between a slowly - growing agricultural economy in its rural hinterland and a more dynamic growth of its own urban economy; between the kinds of available jobs and the aspirations of the existing labour force; and between the output of the formal education system and the job market for educated persons[m]. The study argued that industrial and occupational employment patterns were highly correlated with the geographical and linguistic origins of the working population. This had a notable repercussion for the policy question of for whom jobs are to be created. According to this study, Calcutta's small - scale engineering units might have a good role to play as a supplier of inputs (tube wells, pump sets and other agricultural tools and equipments) to an expanding agricultural sector. The study concluded with the recommendations for implementing some definite measures for the improvement of this sector so that employment in Calcutta can be geared up.

The ILO - WEP city studies concerning Abidjan, Jakarta and Sao - Paolo disclosed the fact that a substantial portion of the workers engaged in small individual enterprises earn less than the workers of the formal sector industries. Besides, a disproportionate share of the additions to the urban working masses, caused by the rural - urban drift, tended to be absorbed into this sort of employment. Most of the city studies placed greater emphasis on the informal sector in their policy solutions.

The major contributions of the ILO - WEP city studies were, the simultaneous evolution of a 'target group' approach to policy recommendations and an identification of the 'working group' as a particular category within the urban economy which resulted in recommendations to increase the volume of employment within particular sectors to the extent of ignoring their position within total structure.

Critiques of the ILO Country Reports

The ILO country reports were all criticised for their "politically utopian recommendations"[n]. In fact, all these reports solicited structural and institutional changes like land reform and fiscal re - distributive policies on such a scale that it was impossible to implement them without any change at the political level.

Colin Leys[o] while criticising the Kenya mission argued that the mission , in considering the situation as capable of being rectified through a programme of reform, misrepresented the actual modes of production in Kenya and their mutual articulation. In his opinion, the mission treated the problem in Kenya as an 'imbalance' and not as 'the contradictory reality'. They failed to see the struggle between oppressing and oppressed classes and wrongly considered only a series of particular 'conflict' of interest which the leadership would resolve[p].

The re-distributive recommendations of the ILO country reports were also challenged on the ground that the groups who were required to make the financial sacrifices were themselves the linkmen of the alliance of domestic and foreign capital.

In addition, the 'target group' approach of the ILO country studies had been criticised due to the failure of the projects to operationalise their earlier contention that "the employment problem could not be seen in isolation. Its position at the centre of the whole development process meant that the employment strategies could only be made sensible within an overall development strategy".[q] It indicates, therefore, the recommendations of the ILO country mission have been criticised for the failure to consider their position within the total economic structure.

Different Conceptualisation of the Informal Sector

We have already mentioned that the informal sector has its conceptual basis in dualistic concept[r] and has been adopted as a policy tool by ILO's target group approach. Their emphasis on informal sector has had a greater impact in shifting research emphasis to the whole gamut of complex activities from which a countable portion of the urban workers earn their livelihood. Gradually, it is being realised that research work on urban economy and employment should not be circled round the modern manufacturing sector alone.

Since the utility of the informal sector is being recognised, researchers and policy makers have applied it to diversity of empirical data and in many different contexts. Consequently, the informal sector has been defined in vivid ways. For example, it has been regarded as synonymous with the urban poor or with people residing at slums or squatter settlements or with the immigrants of the city. In addition, certain kinds of occupations have been enlisted as belonging to the informal sector. It is also interesting to note that it has been regarded at different times that all enterprises, which operate on an illegal basis or violate government rules, are included in the informal sector. Suffice it to say that such wide usage has created too much confusion about this concept.

However, some of the concepts related to informal sector have been originated from Hart's model. Sethuraman[s] explains how the target groups identified in different studies fall into two basic categories. He enumerates them as follows: first: those that are characterised by the level of income of the individuals concerned or by such variables which rest on the income level (such as access to housing or other urban services, adequate foods etc.) and second: those that are based on the variables which determine the income of the individual worker. (For example: personal characteristics, occupational characteristics, status of employment, characteristics of the enterprises on which the worker depends etc.)

A different approach to this concept was contributed by D. Mazumdar[t]. He considers the informal sector as 'unprotected' against the formal 'protected' sector. In his opinion, the distinction between formal and informal sector lies on the assumption that employment in the formal sector is protected so that the workers, in order to get entrance, are supposed to cross the related hurdles. This kind of 'protection' may result from the actions of the trade unions, of the government or of both acting together. He then argues that irrespective of the productivity of the unprotected sector in real terms, in practice, this sector competes poorly with the protected sector in financial terms.

However, for the purpose of reviewing the concept of informal sector, we present some of the studies in the following table. These studies are characterised by using several criteria delineations of formal and informal sector of India.

The diversified criteria used by different studies for spelling out the concept of informal sector was mainly due to the wide spectrum of economic activities that this sector covers as well as the different social relations of production and contexts, under which such studies were carried out.

Characteristics of the Informal Sector

The increase of research work on the urban informal sector has led to a vagueness and inconsistency of definition. The main reason is the lack of a 'clear empirical basis' for the concept. We have mentioned it already that the term 'informal' sector has been used by the practitioners for defining both the enterprises as well as the personnel. The crucial point is, therefore, to decide whether it is the firms or the activities of individual worker that are being considered in this regard.

TABLE: 1:1

Usage of Criteria Relating to Informal Sector

Sr. No.	*Author/ Researcher*	*Study Area (Reference Population Year)*	*Total Population*	*Estimated size as a % of total employment*	*Criteria used*
(1)	(2)	(3)	(4)	(5)	(6)
1:	Joshi & Joshi (1976) 1961	Greater Bombay 1971 41,52,000	59,71,000 47.7 (1)	49.5 (1)	Employment in unorganised sector is a residual of organized sector including all public sector establishments and all privately owned establishments with more than 25 employees.
2:	Deshpande (1979)	Greater Bombay 1961 1971	41,52,000 59,71,000	51.3 (2) 50.4 (2)	Same as above
3:	Bose (1978a)	Calcutta 1971	31,48,746	28.3 (3)	For manufacturing all non-registered units including non-household units (with less than 20 persons) & excluding registered units. For non-manufacturing all units employing 4 or less workers including independent workers.

4:	Papola (1976)	Ahmedabad 1971	16,06,165	46.5 [4]	Workers in units with 10 or less workers and all unattached workers.
5:	Breman (1977)	Valsad District (Gujarat) N.A	75.0 [5]		Informal non-organised workers for the entire district including seasonal migrants.
6:	Mazumdar (1980)	Delhi 1961	23,59,408	61.4 [6]	Residual of workers in all units employing 10 or more workers.
7:	ORG (1978)	Madras Metropolitan Area, 1971	25,00,000	50 - 70 [7]	Workers in all establishments employing 10 or less workers and unattached workers.

SOURCES:

(1) Joshi & Joshi (1976) Table III, p: 48 Er.
(2) Deshpande (1979) Table II, 15, p: 66.
(3) Bose (1978) Table 7, p: 19.
(4) Papola (1978) Table 1.1, p: 12.
(5) Breman (1977) p: 183
(6) Mazumdar (1980) Table 3: p: 25
(7) ORG (1978) p: 46

N.A. = Not Available.

In his dual model, John Keith Hart (1975) made a distinction between income opportunities in wage and self-employment. He considered employment in the formal sector as wage-employment and that of the informal sector as self-employment. The ILO's report on Kenya disclosed the following characteristics of the informal sector[u] "Informal activities are a way of doing things, characterised by (a) ease of entry; (b) reliance on indigenous resources; (c) family ownership of enterprises; (d) small scale of operation; (e) labour intensive and adapted technology; (f) skills acquired outside the formal school system and; (g) unregulated and competitive markets." Besides, according to this report, informal activities are largely ignored and rarely supported; often regulated and sometimes actively discouraged by the governments.

From above, it is evident that the ILO emphasis has been on enterprises supposed to be in the informal sector. The above characteristics, as identified by the ILO, have been questioned by Peattie[v]. In her opinion, a lot of organisations generally exist in the informal sector and possibilities for new entry are differentiated. Therefore, she is reluctant to accept that there is ease of entry in the informal sector. In her words "what seems to characterise these occupations designated as the informal sector, is, therefore, not so much a lack of formal structure, but a diversity and complexity of structure" (p: 24)

Another major criticism of the characteristics of informal sector comes from Breman[w]. He remarked that the decisive factor in getting employment in the informal sector is personal contact. The nature and extent of the network of contacts determines not only whether one is incorporated into the work process but also where and for what type of work. Finally , he concludes , "these different criteria do not cumulate in a clear and consistent stratification." (p: 1906).

Weeks, in his conceptualisation of the formal/informal sector distinction, lays down specific emphasis on the economic insecurity of operation in the informal sector. In his opinion, the formal sector includes government activity itself and all private sector enterprises, which are officially recognised, nurtured and regulated by the state. Numerous measures are seen in the formal sector economic operations: e.g.: tariff and quota protection, import tax rebates, low interest rates etc. While operations in the informal sector are characterised by an absence of such benefits; enterprises and individuals operating outside the systems of benefits and regulations of governments and thus without access to formal credit institutions and sources of transfer of foreign technology, can be enlisted under the informal sector.

Weeks, however, did not agree with the view that these prevailing features make the informal sector static. He considered both formal and informal sector as dynamic in the sense that both of these sectors were continually adapting to external changes. Hence, he also remarked that a dynamic and evolving informal sector was beneficial in many ways provided the relation between formal and informal sector were benign.

On the whole, the characteristics, used to clarify the informal sector concept may be bracketed under the following groups:

First: those characteristics which lay down specific emphasis on the size, ownership, mode of production etc. of the enterprises .

Second: those characteristics which disclose the nature of exchange relationship between the state and the informal sector such as lack of support and recognition from the government, non - existence of credit facility from public institutions etc. and,

Third: those characteristics which are based on the employment situation or labour market processes like easy entrance, self - employment, non - existence of formal agreement for employment etc.

Dificiencies of the Classification Formal/Informal

In sharp contrast to the theoretical formulations put forth by Weeks and the ILO, many of the field studies have pointed out the major deficiencies of the classification formal/ informal. As King[(x)] remarked that "intellectuals have discovered the plight of the working poor , only to decide rather rapidly that unfortunately nothing can be done about it."

However, the major deficiencies of the formal/informal classification are worth emphasizing. These are:

First: It is crude and simple to divide all economic activities into two parts. An ideal outlook is to divide enterprises on a continuum. So as to stress on the intermediate categories as well as the processes of transition along the overall continuum.

Second: The definition of the informal sector, as found in different studies may be confusing enough. So many criteria have been used to define this sector instead of outweighing their relative importance. Yet there is no appropriate guideline for classifying such activities having some common feature of both informal and formal sector.

Third: Instead of being two separate and independent sector it is more likely to be the case that they are in a constant changing state of interaction and that one sector may be dominated or created by the other sector.

Fourth: It would be a gross mistake to apply a particular policy for launching development to the whole informal sector. For example, in order to finance the informal slum units of Calcutta, a co - operative amongst those units can be formed. But the same policy will not sound well for those informal units scattering all over Calcutta. Therefore, in order to counter with the wideness and diversity of this sector, it would be wise to implement different sets of policy measures.

Fifth: There is a peculiar trend, as commonly depicted in the literature, to consider the informal sector as exclusively urban while the analogous activities in the rural areas have been described in some other terms like 'rural traditional units' etc. Also the rural part of the informal sector receives less attention. This is unjustified. The term 'informal' sector should logically include both parts, so as to enlighten the existence of identical activities and equal situations in the rural areas. Besides, the related essays in this context, "...fail to clarify what the other components of the total national system actually are.[y].

Sixth: Some of the analysts hold a pessimistic view about the future of informal sector. They make the delimitation between formal and informal sector by such criteria as absence of government support and recognition. But, the underlying mistake is, the informal character will be no longer present, as soon as the government assists and recognises this sector. According to the opinion of these analysts, government support is virtually a guarantee of success. This is simply overlooking some basic facts. In the practical field, there is a complex, competitive and subordinate relationship between large and small enterprises. The monopolists have in their armoury wide range strategies for out placing the small competitors, [z] (e.g.: differential pricing, 'media pressure' on consumers etc.) against which government support alone could provide a little help.

Seventh: Another inconsequent tendency is to intermingle neighbourhoods, household, people and activities with enterprises. It is doubtful whether this two - sector concept is applicable at all for those people who work in both sectors at different stages in their life cycle, times of the year or even times of the same day. Problem may also arise, if some one applies this concept to household or neighbourhood. Because some members may earn their livelihood from formal sector while others from informal sector. Again, it is questionable whether this dual approach should be applied to activities, as both formal and informal sector firms may carry out the identical activity.

Eighth: Some of the followers of dualistic concept even

consider 'urban informal sector' and 'urban poor' as synonymous. This is a simple fallacy. It is not always true that all poor people work in the informal sector; nor it is a fact that all persons who work in the informal sector are poor. In many countries of the third world, there are countable numbers of low - paid formal sector workers.

Ninth: Even if, we accept the two - sector terminology, it is still doubtful how far the official programmes aim at the amelioration of informal sector could provide real benefit. The paradox of the situation is that the recommended policy changes will inevitably be detrimental to an elite, who is responsible for its execution.

Finally, it can be argued that the characteristics that constitute the basis of the formal-informal sector distinction represent a pattern of continuous variation in a typical LDC labour market and, therefore, the dichotomy is unwarranted.

Validity of the Dualistic Concept

The deficiencies listed above do not imply that the dualistic concept is totally irrelevant. It is useful if the conceptual distinctions amongst different sub sector "a policy - oriented discussion of the dynamic interactions between different sub sectors and the changes that could be expected to follow specific developments." [AA]

Besides, we think that all of the failings of the dualistic concept might be remedied by greater clarity and rigour in the use of the formal/informal terminology and by the development of appropriate subdivisions within the two sectors.

The formal / informal sectoral classifications are good buckets to keep together and to focus attention upon, particular groups of activities and the voluminous research on the informal sector has added to our knowledge of many comparatively little known economic activities. Therefore, we might as well use this concept and terminology until something better comes along.

Conclusion

The theoretical basis of the informal sector has been deeply rooted into the dualistic concept. It has been used in the ILO's target group approach as a policy tool. The influence of the ILO's emphasis on the informal sector has drawn many researches into this particular field. The conceptual development of the informal sector concerns three fundamental areas: these are, the features of the informal sector, its articulation with the rest of the urban economy and the differentiations within the informal sector itself.

However, due to the inherent major deficiencies of the formal / informal classification, it is needless to mention that there should be more studies in different urban areas which might bring forth workable, locally relevant and comparatively logical definition of the informal sector so as to enable others to have a better understanding about this sector.

REFERENCES

(a). Lewis W.A.: (1954): "Economic Development with unlimited supplies of Labour" in *Manchester School*, Vol. XII, No. 2. October 1954, pp. 1239 - 1261.

(b). Fei. J. and Ranis, G (1964) : *Development of the labour surplus Economy : Theory and Policy*, (Homewood IV, Richard Erwin, 1964).

(c). Hart, K (1973): "Informal Income Opportunities and Urban Employment in Ghana" in *Journal of Modern African Studies,* March, 1973. Vol. 18, Issue: 3, pp: 521 - 537.

(d). Weeks, J (1975): "Policies for Expanding Employment in the Informal Urban Sector of Developing Economies" in *International Labour Review,* January, 1975, Vol. - III, No.1, p. 17.

(e). ILO: (1972), "Employment, Incomes and Equality: A Strategy for Increasing Productive Employment in Kenya", Geneva.

(f). ILO: (1972), *ibid.,* p. XI.

(g). ILO: (1970): *Towards Full Employment: A Programme for Colombia*: Geneva.

(h). Besides, the Colombia mission has differentiated amongst open unemployment, disguised unemployment and under employment. Open unemployment: persons without work and seeking it; Disguised unemployment: persons without work and who would probably seek it if unemployment were much lower; open under employment: persons working less than 32 hours per week and seeking to work longer; Disguised under employment: persons working less than 32 hours per week who would probably seek longer hours if the opportunity were available.

(i). ILO: (1970), *ibid.,* p. 21.

(j) ILO : (1970), *ibid.,* p. 21.

(k) This summary is based on the analysis made by Thorbecke. E: "The Employment Problem: a critical evaluation of four comprehensive country reports" in ILO, strategy for employment promotion *op. cit.*

(l) ILO: (1975), *"Calcutta, its urban development and employment prospects"*. Geneva.

(m) ILO: (1975), *ibid.,* p. 97.

(n) Leys. C(1975) "Under development in Kenya : The political Economy of Neo - Colonialism : '64 - '71" : p. 260, (London, Heinemann, '75).

(o) Leys. C (1973) "Interpreting African underdevelopment: reflections on the ILO report on employment, incomes and equality in Kenya" African Affairs: Vol. 72 (1973), p. 419 - 429.

(p) Leys. C (1975), *ibid.*, p. 264.

(q) Moser. C: (1977): "The Informal sector or petty commodity Production? Autonomy or Dependence in Urban Development, DPU, working paper, No: 3.

(r) This is why informal sector and formal sector have been considered by many writers as: Two juxtaposed systems of production, one derived from capitalist mode of production, the other from the peasant system (T.G. McGee: "Peasants in cities: a paradox, a paradox, a most ingenious paradox": Human organisation: and 'a bazaar type economy' (C. Geertz: Peddlers and Prices: social change and economic modernisation in two Indonesian towns: Chicago : University of Chicago press : '63) as two circuits : the upper and lower circuits (M. Santos : "Economic Development and Urbanisation in Underdeveloped countries : the two circuits of the urban economy and their spatial implications" unpublished manuscript '73) and as two sectors 'a high profit/high wage international oligopolistic sector and a low profit/low wage competitive capitalistic sector' (M.B. Brown : The economics of imperialism : Harmondsworth :Penguin '74).

(s) Sethuraman, S.V. (1976) "The urban informal sector: concept, measurement and policy" *International Labour Review:* Vol. 114 (1976), p. 74.

(t) Mazumdar D (1976) "The urban informal sector": Washington D.C.: World Bank staff working paper: No. 211 (1975). See also, Mazumdar D: "The urban informal sector": *World Development*, Vol. 4 (1976), pp. 655 - 679.

(u) ILO: (1972), *Employment, Incomes and Equality: op. cit.*, p. 6.

(v) Peattie L.R. : (1980) : "Anthropological Perspective on the Concepts of Dualism, the Informal Sector and Marginality in Developing Urban Economics" in *International Regional Science Review :* Vol. 5, No. 1, pp. 1 - 29.

(w) Breman (1976): "A Dualistic Labour System: A critique of the 'Informal Sector' Concept" in *Economic and Political Weekly*, Nov. 27, Dec. 4, Dec. 11, 1976.

(x) King, K: (1974): "Kenya's Informal Machine Maker: a study of small - scale industry in Kenya's emergent artisan society" in *World Development*, Vol. 2, No. S: 4/5 March, 1974, p. 10.

(y) Bromley, R [1989] " The Urban Informal Sector: Why is it worth discussing"? in The Urban Informal Sector ed. By Bromely Ray, (London, Carfax Publishing Co, 1989), p. 1034.

(z) See for example, Oliveira, F.De (1972) " A economia brasileira: critica a razao dualista." *Estudos Cebrap.* No. 2 (Oct. '72), p. 3.

(aa) Standing Guy (1977): "Urban /workers and patterns of Employment" in Studies of urban labour market behaviour in development areas ed. By Kannapan. S. p. 37.

2

A Close Look at Some of the Major Informal Industries in Calcutta*

In this chapter, we have delineated some of the major informal industries in Calcutta. These are: the tailoring industry in Garden Reach of west Calcutta, the tanneries in Tangra and Tiljala of south-east Calcutta, the scattered plastic industry of all over Calcutta, the timber and plywood industry in Ultadanga of north-east Calcutta and the clay modelling industry in Kumartuli of north Calcutta.

PREAMBLE: THE CASE OF CALCUTTA

The conceptual framework of the informal sector may be overhauled in the case of Calcutta. The main question is the following: at the level of the firm where can one delineate a limit between formal and informal sector as defined in the previous chapter? Indian legislation has a convenient separation: the Factories Act applies, indeed to establishments employing 10 workers or more. In a first approximation, all units below 10 employees could be considered as belonging to informal sector. But another type of registration exits: the registration as small scale industry with the State Directorate of Cottage and small scale Industries which enables them to have access to

---

* We find it logical to keep the surveyed data intact so as to stimulate a sense of originality. The indices of the current period, however, have been noted under the 'REFERENCES'.

various advantages as part of the state promotion policy. A minimal delimitation of the informal sector can be adopted: units non-registered with DCSSI or under Factories Act. To this non-factory forms of work should be added: household industry, specially in slums, is wide-spread. Yet such a definition of informal sector is very restrictive; for example, what is the difference between two identical units in similar activities, one registered and the other non-registered? The former is entitled to some benefits, which the owner of the latter will not try to obtain because of complicated procedures or long delays. One has then envisage other differentiating factors:

- Places of the unit. A large number of units are located in the 3000 slums enumerated in Calcutta. Numerous activities take place there. It can, therefore, be considered that slums industries belong to the informal sector but non-registered units are also to be found in other places.
- How far does the unit owner fix his prices and control the outlets of his products? Does he depend on middlemen (dealers, vendors, mahajans or dadandars) who impose on him a low price hardly covering his direct costs (especially, raw materials purchased at a high price) , the low wages of his workers notwithstanding a profit margin?
- Do wages rates paid by the unit conform to the "protected sector" or do they only enable the workers to live at the bare subsistence level, even if government has enacted minimum wages legislation?

The following examples of some of the Calcutta's informal sector industries will be examined in the light of the theoretical framework of the preceding chapter and the questions just arise.

CALCUTTA'S INFORMAL SECTORS

A. The Tailoring Industries

Garden Reach, in west Calcutta and the adjoining villages of the district of 24 parganas are synonymous with tailoring industry in the same way as Howrah is associated with engineering industries and even more. Walking in the area reveals the amazing fact that almost every house shelters people Working on one or several sewing machines. It is estimated that more than one lakh of people earn their living directly out of the clothing industry in the area, and if one takes into account people who depend on it indirectly (shops selling cloth, thread and buttons, transporters of cloth or ready-made garments, etc.) in all two lakhs of people are closely connected with this industry.

The industry is predominantly Muslim: 90% of the tailors are of this religion. The industry dates back to the middle of the 19th century when the Nawab Wazed Ali and some of his followers settled down in what was then known as "METIABRUZ" [(a)]. They came from Lucknow where they had been tailors and they introduced their traditional trade in their new settlement. To the families already settled in the area before independence were added the refugees of the former East Pakistan who were trained tailors in their own villages or towns and took to their traditional activity on settling down in Garden Reach. At the time of undivided Bengal, the province was famous for its fabrics, coming either from Dacca (muslin) or from Metiabruz, which is now more or less confounded with Garden Reach. Unfortunately, it has not been possible to find out the turnover of the industry over the period and even an estimation of today's turnover is very difficult to make, as there is no centralized authority or association to collect and compute the figures.

The value of the garments exported from India in '80 was Rs. 3.598 million. According to the Apparels Export Promotion Council, New Delhi, 2.6% only of this value originated from Calcutta (Rs. 93.5 million). The percentages were 57.5% for Delhi, 26.2% for Bombay, 6% for Madras and 5.7% for Bangalore. The tailoring industry in Garden Reach caters then mainly to the needs of the eastern region and does not export much compared to Delhi and Bombay. But though the industry has been established in Garden Reach for many years, it retains most of the characteristics of an informal sector industry.

Let us first study the salient features of the industry before stressing the factors which make it belong to the informal sector and then see what are the main needs of the industry to improve its working as well as the conditions of its most deprived workers.

(a) Features

The tailoring industry in Garden Reach has a very complex structure, depending on the types of jobs done, the relations between the different operators, the size of units etc. The variations of structure and relationship would take months to study but there are a few common features that can be underlined as follows:

— Basically, the industry is divided into three levels,

which compose a three-tier system. At the top are situated the cloth merchants of Barabazar who control the main input of the industry: cloth, alone, accounts for no less than 75% to 80% of the cost price of most of the garments made in Garden Reach. Therefore, those who control its price have the "commanding heights" over the tailoring industry as a whole.

The "ostagars" or unit owner represents the second tier. The ostagars do not form a homogenous lot. They are divided into three categories, though the line of separation is fairly blurred. The big ostagars, numbering less than fifty, have an annual turnover above Rs. 5 lakhs. They give work to at least twenty tailors. The small ostagars are mostly self-employed, or may have one or two hired tailors. In between are the middle ostagars whose turnover may vary from one to several lakhs and who give work to five to fifteen tailors. The smaller units may employ as few as three to five tailors. The larger, over hundred. The number of ostagars is impossible to assess: there is a high degree of mobility amongst them as the most successful tailors can become ostagars and the other way round, the impoverished ostagars can revert to the condition from which they had risen: tailors. The ostagars procure the orders as well as the raw materials, distribute the work between their workers, secure the payments etc.

Lastly, the tailor themselves constitute the third tier. The word 'Tailor' in fact encompasses a whole range of occupation in the clothing industry: supervisors, designer, cutter, tailor, snitcher, button holes makers, button fixer, trimmer, measurer, ironer, helper, packer, machine mechanics. The tailors are daily wage earners: they are generally paid half the amount due at the end of the day and the balance after one week. They are paid at piece-rates.

— The lists of these occupations bring to light another feature of the garment making industry: the extreme job specialisation, which allows a higher productivity and lessens the labour charges. Whereas in New Market for example, a pair of trousers would be made entirely by one single tailor; in Garden Reach, the same operation involves at least five different workers; the cutter, the machine-man, two hand-layers who prepare the work for the machine-man, the button-fixer and the trimmer. Similarly, whereas ten to fifteen years ago, garments were made accordingly to individual measurement, the steady increase in the demand due to the natural demographic growth and to the rise of the purchasing power of the urban middle class and rural rich farmers has led the industry to manufacture in series rather than individual high quality pieces.

— The labour relations are of a non-organised nature. There is no direct link of employment; most units are non-registered, do not have any deeds or any system of accounts. They run as family businesses, which are transmitted from generation to generation through successive divisions between sons. The tailors work on a verbal contract basis for one or several ostagars who supply orders to them. They may work in the premises of the ostagars or in their own houses, helped by unpaid family labours. The situation arising out of this loose structure of employment is one of great fludity and flexible, which works to the advantage of the ostagars but to the disadvantage of tailors. The latter have to bear the seasonality of the market, which is directly reflected, in the number of orders. Practically, work is assured for six months a year: three months at the time of the Hindu festival of Durga Puja (from August to October) and three months from February to April which is the season for weddings and the time of the Bengali Naba Barsa (New year).

— Another characteristic of the profession is a complicated credit structure involving several middlemen. Most of the ostagars do not have enough working capital to enable them to finance the making of bulk quantities of garments right from the purchase of cloth till the receipt of the payment from the buyer. They have to resort to credit. The first source of credit is the cloth merchant of Bara Bazar. The longer the credit, the dearer the cloth is :If the credit is for one week, the price is higher by 5% than when it is paid in cash; for two weeks by 10%; for one month, by 15%. The actual interest rate of this non-institutional system of credit is as high as 180% p.a. in the most favourable case. Usually the proceeds of the sales on the weekly haats enable the ostagar to repay every week the largest part of the credit for the cloth he had purchased in the previous week. The outstanding part of the credit is paid at the end of the Bengali year (April).

On the other hand, the ostagars who execute government orders (Uniforms for police force, Calcutta Port Trust, government department or public undertakings) do not receive them directly. Some well established contractors in Calcutta get the government tenders, quote and then farm out the orders to the real manufacturers, the ostagars. In this case they are subcontractors against the payment of a commission of 15% to the contractor who has procured the order. These contractors act not only as marketing agents but also as credit suppliers. When the ostagars go to Barabazar to purchase the cloth required to execute the order, the bill is paid cash by the contractor in whose name the order has been placed. This advance is adjusted at the time of the final payment when the government has paid the contractor : the ostagars will receive the contracted price less the advance paid on his behalf by the contractor and less the commission. Thus, compared to the cloth merchants of Barabazar such contractors play the double role of supplying a market and the corresponding credit (or part of it). But their remuneration is still exorbitantly high.

— Besides, jobs on order, either from government or from shops in Calcutta, the main marketing outlets are the 'haats' or open-air wholesale markets. Two smaller haats are held twice a week: Harishah haat on Sundays and Wednesday, Chetla haat on Saturdays and Wednesdays. They are mainly meant for the local markets of Calcutta and West Bengal.

The larger haat and the older as well, is the Mongola haat[(b)] held once a week on Tuesday near Howrah Maidan. Buyers at Howrah haat come not only from Calcutta or West Bengal but also from neighbouring states and from distant cities like Bombay, Delhi or Madras. Huge transactions are made there every week. Most of the ostagars manage to get a stall to display their products, as they depend entirely on the haat for selling them. It belongs to private owners who, charge very high rates for the stalls: the "Salami" or outright, under-the-table payment demanded to rent the best-located stalls might reach Rs. 50,000/-. The business is mostly transacted in cash, which the smaller ostagars badly need to be able to carry on their operations of the week to come. Generally, direct relations are established between buyers and sellers but another middleman may interfere: he is known as 'gadhiwalla' and commits himself to find the goods desire by a buyer who comes to his 'gadhi' in Barabazar or elsewhere and thus does not have to find the seller himself. A commission of 6% contributed equally by the buyer and the seller pays the gadhiwalla.

— A last characteristic of tailoring industry in Garden Reach is the geographical specialisation, which is very striking when one, walks there. One area specialises in trousers, another in shirts, a third one in babies' garments, a fourth one in maxis and girls or ladies dresses, etc.

It is very difficult to know the cost structure of the trade. Not only wide variation exits, depending on the types of garments made, the reputation of the ostagars and the size of the units but prices and costs are kept secret and one has to crosscheck figures before coming to a satisfactory results. As already mentioned, the prices depend to a great extent on the prices of cloth. The 'favour' one enjoys amongst one or several Marwari cloth merchants of Barabazar will enable the lucky ostagars to get a slight rebate compared to his fellowmen. The labour charges usually represent less than 20% of the selling price. In a midi or girls dress for example, the selling price of which is Rs. 17/-, the labour charges come to Rs. 2.75/-: Re. 1/- for the cutter, Re. 1/-for the machine man, 50 paise for the two hand layers, 15 paise for the button-hole maker and 10 paise for the trimmer. The profit of the ostagar is said to be not more than 50 paise for such a garment (3% of the selling price). For an ostagar who owns four machines, each served by a chain of four workers and who would make only this type of garments, the daily profit comes to Rs. 40/-, (considering that a chain of tailors can make twenty pieces a day) which is double the daily wage of the cutter or the machine man.

In another example, quoted by an informant, the labour charges for one dozen of ordinary frocks would be Rs. 12/- A machine man assisted by one helper can make two dozens within eight hours. Their wages would then come to Rs. 24/

-: Rs. 15/- for the machine man and Rs. 9/- for the helper. It seems there are wide variation in the rates: some women may earn as little as Rs. 5/- per day whereas experienced machine man or cutter may earn Rs. 15/- to Rs. 25/- per day. However, one has to keep in mind the fact that these rates are supposed to remunerate unpaid family labour as well.

Many more examples should be taken to come to a conclusion on the profitability of the industry and the respective incomes of large ostagars, small ostagars and tailors. In certain cases the ostagars might even sell on Howrah haat a part of their weekly production at a loss when the fashion is changed or especially when they are in need of cash for the production of the week to come.

In the recent years, it seems that whereas the prices of cloth, thread, hooks and other accessories have gone up, the rates of labour have remained more or less stagnant. The industry in Garden Reach has to face the competition of more mechanised industries especially in South India. The prices of ready-made garments have to remain low if Garden Reach wants to maintain its position on the Indian market as a whole. This can be achieved only at the expense of the tailors who have to accept low wages.

(b) Reviewing the Informal Sector Criteria

The basic features of the tailoring industry in Garden Reach make it a part of the sprawling informal sector of Calcutta's metropolitan economy. Though the concept of

Informal sector has had varying definitions and a great deal of controversy still exists about it, the clothing industry conforms to the main criteria of the informal sector as laid down by several studies of the ILO and other international institutions:

— The industry is labour-intensive. The investment in fixed capital is low, restricted to a few sewing machines. On the other hand, the amount of working capital is high.

— Most of the units are proprietorship and family concerns. The whole family is usually involved in the work: men as machine man, snitchers, cutters or helpers and women as button-hole makers, button snitchers or even too, machine man; children carry out various non specialised tasks.

— The market is highly competitive and very fluctuating. Work is not permanent and there is no job security. Seasonal peaks, specially at the time of the Hindu Durga Puja, force the ostagars who can afford it to lock up substantial amount of working capital in inventories; those who cannot raise the necessary finance miss the best market opportunities of the year. The adjustment to the market conditions has to be borne by the workers themselves, for with the piece-rate system of wage payment no work is equal to no pay. There is a very little amount of workers-protection by trade unions, as they are scattered around in small units and it is difficult to organise them. One trade union, West Bengal's Tailors Union affiliated to CITU has met with a relative amount of success while organising the tailors of Moistalla, an area adjacent to Garden Reach. However, the Union has not been successful in Metiabruz, as the structure of the industry, according to an informant, is more intricated and less conducive to trade unionism than in Moistalla.

— Access to the industry is mostly done at very early ages, by training on-the-job totally independently from the formal system of schooling. From their very childhood, children start helping their guardians: The future of the child is thus sacrificed to the immediate present when the need is to send to work more family members so as to increase the income. A young boy needs something like three years of non-paid training before being entitled to remuneration. After the training and the moral commitment of staying for a minimum period with the ostagar who has provided it are over, there is a high degree of labour mobility. Workers try to improve their earnings and their status by shifting from one ostagar to the other and by climbing up the scale of skills.

— As observed earlier, credit is provided mostly by non-institutional sources of finance at very high rates of interest. The large number of middlemen operating at different levels deprives the workers of the fruit of their labour and the ostagars of the control over the main levers of the market.

(c) Immediate Needs

In conclusion, there is room for improving the working of the industry and the lot of the smaller ostagars and the tailors. The most urgent requirement is bank credit at usual bank rates, which will enable the unit owners to by pass the middlemen suppliers of credit. In '75-'76, the CMDA conducted a survey in the area with a view of identifying small ostagars and recommending their cases to nationalized banks for finance. It seems that not much came out of it, the report of the survey itself having not been published. More recently, banks came into the picture, specially the Bank of Baroda with its Multi Service Agency which has introduced a simplified and fast procedure of lending: lending is purpose-oriented instead of security oriented, the paper work has been brought to a minimum, the security and guarantee abolished. The ostagars of Garden Reach were the first to benefit from the new scheme of this agency established in '74. The amount lent to about 800 of them, totaling Rs. 16 lakhs, has enabled them to constitute inventories in preparation for the peaks of festive seasons, but it is still small compared to the needs of the area. It seems that other banks have not been able to adapt their complicated lending procedures to the informal state of most units and low education level of their owners. They still demand Balance Sheets and P&L A/C, whereas most ostagars do not maintain systematic accounts.

A second need expressed by ostagars is that the government or government owned undertakings should place their orders directly with the ostagars and not with contractors who are not the real manufactures. This would enable the ostagars to increase their earnings by 15%, which is the amount of the commission paid to contractors.

Another need, too, is to lessen the dependency of the ostagars on Barabazar for the supply of cloth. Cloth and thread should be supplied directly to them from government mills.

Basically, a minimum amount of co-operation between ostagars would enable them to be heard and considered as one of the bargaining forces on the competitive market of the garment making industry. One of the possible roles of the Calcutta Municipal Corporation in this area might be to act as kind of catalyst so as to bring about the so much needed co-operation. The Calcutta Municipal Corporation could also be instrumental in gathering reliable data on the industry so as to pursue its case with the government, the banks and other institutions, which may come forward for assistance.

B. The Tanneries

Tanning raw hides and skins and leather industries are sizeable industries in Calcutta. They predominate in the eastern outskirts of the city. Besides tanneries located in Tangra and Tiljala, it is estimated that 90% of the working population of Entally and Phoolbagan depend on leather for their livelihood. Without going into the details of the structure of this trade, let us mention a few points, which make it, confirm to the informal sector[c].

The employment situation is very mobile: employment, first, is seasonal. During the monsoon when work has to stop, many unit owners, who originate from Bihar where their families still live, go back to their villages in order to take part in the busy agricultural season. This aspect illustrates the linkage between immigration and informal sector. Then, there is no clear-cut distinction between unit-owners and workers. A unit, indeed, consists of one of several pits, rented in most cases, where hide and skin tanning is carried out. To be an owner depends on the finance one can get and this is a reversible situation. A survey conducted in view of writing one of the reports mentioned below states that out of one hundred workers, fifty-two had worked earlier as unit-owners.

Lack of capital to purchase raw skins is a major constraint. Very few owners, except those who own the pits, have enough capital at their command to be able to work through out the year. The second part estimates that seventy-five percent of them are compelled to borrow funds from moneylenders at a minimum rate of 5% p.m. The authors mention the rules governing small loans: for a loan of Rs. 100/-, Rs. 4/- is deducted right when the loan is disbursed. Repayment is within nine weeks, at the rate of 12.5% per week. Other lenders are the owners of large-scale tanneries and the customers. In the latter case, interest is paid through a rebate in the final price.

Sale of processed skin is entirely in the hands of 'Dadandars' or speculative merchants who purchase the products from the tanneries at low prices and resell them with a very substantial margin.

An interesting statistical table covering five hundred small-scale unit owners clearly shows that investment of capital makes the owners monthly incomes higher.

TABLE 1.2

Some Useful Information about the Small Tanners

Capital Size (Rs.)	*Number of Tanners*	*Monthly Income (Rs.) Less than*
Less than 200	200	100
200-1000	50	275
1000-2000	50	350
2000-4000	100	600
More than 5000	100	800

[*Source* : J. Basu Roy Chowdhury & Dr. T.H. Thomas A scheme for resettlement of small tanners, 1977].

The income of sixty percent of the tanners are lower than Rs. 350/-p.m., the average income being Rs. 382.50. No data is available on the average of workers wages.

This summary study of small scale tanneries brings then to the fore employment seasonality, the role of middlemen for marketing and money lenders at exorbitant rates, as well as the low incomes which are all characteristics of an informal sector industry.

C. The Plastic Industries

This industry illustrates the contrast existing between organised sector factories (which make about 70% of the total number of plastic processing units in Calcutta) and the informal sector units. The industry provides employment to thirty thousand persons directly and twenty thousand persons indirectly.[d] It has progressed at a fast pace: the low capital required (a manual injection machines cost less than Rs. 2000/-) attracted many entrepreneurs to venture into this recent industry.

The main finished products are consumers' domestic goods (combs, ball-pens, buckets, caps, sandals, toys, soap-cases etc.) and packaging items (bags, bottles, sheets etc.).

Informal sector units, which number around one thousand in Calcutta's agglomeration, can hardly balance their costs; 80% of the cost price of a finished product is due to the cost of raw material. Small units have been hit doubly by the rise caused by the hike of petroleum and naphtha products; they do not have enough working capital to purchase them against cash payments and final demand has dwindled following the price-hike. Difference between units of the two sectors is noticeable not only as far as working capital is concerned, but also in the marketing net work: formal sector units have an organised distribution network, as the larger ones have agencies in Calcutta and outside Bengal and the others have appointed whole sellers and retailers. Informal sector units depend on one market in Calcutta: Bagri market, the conditions of which are dictated to the unit owners by middlemen.

The West Bengal government recently enacted minimum wages legislation applicable to the plastic industries located in the state. Since May '79, the basic rates were as follows:

Unskilled worker: Rs. 8.38 for 8 working hours
Semiskilled worker: Rs. 9.46 " " "
Skilled worker: Rs. 11.73 " " "
(*SOURCE:* Indian Plastic Federation)

To the basic salary is added a D.A. adjusted twice a year according to the consumer's price index. Larger units can implement this legislation but informal sector workers have to be content with wages as low as Rs. 3/- to Rs. 5/- per day.

One can still go a degree further in the 'informality' of the plastic industry when mentioning jobs executed by household workers, specially women whose wages are still lower than informal sector unit workers. This extreme degree of exploitation is mainly to be found in slums: a family we visited was assembling plastic whistles for a piece rate wages as low as Rs. 1.40/- per day. Recycling plastic waste is a sizeable activity connected with plastic industry that is carried out mainly by slum children.

D. The Timber and Plywood Industries[e]

The location of timber and plywood industry is mainly concentrated on both sides of the canal of Ultadanga of north east Calcutta as well as some of the roads ad-joining the canal. Such geographical concentration is mainly explained by the locational advantage of hitherto navigable canal, used in transportation of timber logs from distant areas. These units/free of cost have used the vacant land.

Through discussion and visit to the locality, the total numbers of productive units were estimated to be in the range of 200-250 units. In order to have a clear view, different sizes of units have been verified.

Some of the units were reluctant to furnish any data. Many a unit do not maintain records or registers. Therefore, the analytical part of our study is concerned only with those units where complete information is available. These units have been categorized according to their volume of capital. This is shown in the following table:

TABLE 1.3

Distribution of the Units by Capital Structure

Group	*Total Capital (Rs.)*	*Number of Units*	*% Distribution*
A	1-5,000	17	11.33
B	5,001-40,000	68	45.33
C	40,001-1,00,000	45	30.00
D	Above 1,00,000	20	13.34
Total		150	100.00

It is observed that about 40% of the units were set up during '71-'75, covering the last three years of the 4th Five Year Plan and first two years of the 5th Five Year Plan. There has been a steady rate of growth of these industries from '61. The units in GROUP – A are smallest by virtue of their being late entrants to the business.

The ownership structure of these units is shown in the table below.

TABLE 1.4

Structure of Ownership

Group

Type	*A*	*B*	*C*	*D*	*Total*
Proprietary	16	55	25	13	112
Partnership	1	13	17	6	37
Co-Operative	—	—	—	1	1
Total	17	68	45	20	150

It is observed that about 75% of the units are proprietary units and the rest is partnership with only one co-operative unit. In each group about 65% of the units are 'proprietary' in nature.

About 50% of the units have indicated their business to be seasonal in nature. During rainy season, from June to September, timber, the major input to the plywood industry, falls in short supply. Moreover, sun drying of veneers, required for manufacturing of plywood, is affected adversely, due to rain. However, the seasonality affects the smaller units more. For the larger units, the volume of activities is more or less same throughout the year. The volume of employment is similarly affected.

None of the units in GROUP-A are registered with SSI/SISI. 26 out of 68, 21 out of 45 and 14 out of 20 are SSI/SISI registered units in GROUP-B, C and D respectively.

(a) Production Activities/Input-Output

There are broadly four categories of productive units: (1) Some units are engaged in production of wooden packing boxes and planks. These units consume timber as major raw material input. Cutting of such timber, to attain different shapes, is done with the help of sawing machine. There are other types of cutting machines too. These units are known as timber industry; (2) Some units are engaged in manufacturing plywood. These units consume timber logs as major initial raw material input. Timbers are placed on the peeling machine and veneer comes out of the process.

Veneers are then boiled and sent to either mechanical drier or open land for drying up by virtue of mechanical energy or sunshine. Dried veneers are then put to gluing machines for pasting of few leaves together to make a set of plywood. Hydraulic machine is also used for pressing the veneers. The plywood is manufactured for making tea chests. The quality of this plywood must strictly conform to the specification 15:10, laid down by the Indian Standard Institute. Plywood not conforming to this specification is meant for other multi-farious uses, mainly for manufacturing packing boxes for pharmaceuticals and other industries; (3) There are some units, which are engaged in manufacturing veneer only. These units are fully dependent on the units manufacturing the finished product i.e. plywood. Veneer is, therefore, in the nature of intermediate goods. The units belonging to GROUP-A dominate this activity; (4) Some units are engaged in manufacturing plywood from veneer, through stages as mentioned above.

It is further observed that 86% of the total value of output of GROUP –A units is meant for tea industries. This high percentage is due to the fact that most of the units in this group cater to the needs of plywood manufacturing units. In this connection, it may be noted again that most of the units in this group produce veneer, an intermediate good, which are ultimately required for manufacturing of tea chest and other packing boxes.

Approximately 49% and 40% of the total value of output of GROUP-B and GROUP-C units respectively are meant for manufacturing of tea chests and plywood shooks required in tea industries.

About 63% of the total value of output of GROUP-D units is meant for manufacturing of tea chests for tea industries. This is because of the fact that most of the large units are approved units of the Indian Standard Institution. Any unit manufacturing plywood for tea chests must be an approved unit of ISI, subject to its meeting certain conditions as laid down by the ISI and these conditions can only be met by unit with larger capital base.

The units in GROUP-A belong to the lowest capital class hold the smallest quantum of land space (776 sq.ft. per unit) and the units in GROUP-D, belong to the largest capital groups, holding maximum land space (17,913 sq. ft. per unit). It may be noted that there exists a positive correlation between the amount of capital and holding of land space.

(b) Labour

The total number of workers, inclusive of factory and office staff is 1423. It is observed that GROUP-A employs 5% of the total work force, due to its dearth of capital as well as dearth of land space. GROUP-D, the owner of largest share of capital employs only 23% of the work force due to its technology being capital intensive in nature.

Besides, it has been noticed that as the capital base increases, the proportion of unskilled and casual labour falls and the proportion of skilled and permanent labour rise. A fraction, however small of unskilled labours, in addition to all 'skilled' labours, is employed on 'permanent' basis.

All the workers and even majority of the office staff is non-matriculate. Majority of the workers engaged in sawing activities are of South Indian origin, though they have settled in West Bengal permanently.

About 92% of the total labour force, as found through physical verification, belong to the wage class of Rs. 100/- to Rs. 349/- p.m. In addition, it is also found that the wage structure of GROUP-B and GROUP-C are almost equal. The weighted average wage p.m. in different groups are given in the following table.

TABLE 1.5

Weighted Average Wage

	Gr. A	*Gr. B*	*Gr. C*	*Gr. D*
Weighted average wage Per labour per month :	204.10	218.16	221.04	236.77

It is evident from above that the larger is the size of the unit, the higher is the average (weighted) wage per labour per month.

(c) Raw Materials

Timber is the major raw materials for timber and plywood units. There are about 108 species of timber usable in these units. As regard source of input, it is observed that 79% of the total timber input, consumed by all the four groups of industries together are obtained from within the state of West Bengal (particularly from North Bengal).

About 90% of the timber consumed by these industries are procured from middlemen operating in the locality.

As regards other raw material input i.e. Gluing chemicals, mainly required in the plywood manufacturing units, it is to point out that total cost of the same is very insignificant, compared to the total cost of production. These gluing chemicals are mainly produced from within West Bengal.

(d) Capital

In course of survey, it is found that the requirement of working capital is more in case of small units than that of large units. While analysing the source of capital, it is seen that major part of the finance is own mobilised capital. This is indicative of high rate of capitalisation of corporate profits. The incidence of bank/institutional finance is very negligible. The sources of capital are exhibited in the following table:

TABLE 1.6

Sourcewise Distribution of Borrowed Capital

Source	*Gr. A (Rs.)*	*Gr. B (Rs.)*	*Gr. C (Rs.)*	*Gr. D (Rs.)*	*Total (Rs.)*
Bank	—	43,000	2,57,500	3,25,000	6,25,500
Non-banking financial intermediaries	5,600	39,500	1,16,700	6,81,000	8,42,800
Total	5,600	82,500	3,74,200	10,06,000	14,68,300

From the above table, the following comments can be made:

(1) Bank financing is absent from small units; (2) The greater is the volume of bank financing, the larger is the

size of the units; (3) The larger units depend on non-bank finance to a great extent due to limitations in the availability of bank credits.

Highlighting the different facets of disposal of finished goods, it has been observed that (1) Self-marketing is more prevalent amongst the smaller units. The larger is the unit, the greater is %age of marketing made through middle men; (2) Greater proportion of finished products of smaller units flow to CMDA zone as well as to the zone outside CMDA but within West Bengal and vice-versa. The greater %age of finished product of larger units flow to areas outside West Bengal, as compared with the %age of output of smaller units flowing to outside West Bengal. That is, the extent of market is wide to the larger units; (3) There is positive association between %age of output flowing to outside West Bengal and %age of output carried by railways; (4) on an average 90% of the output is transported by road.

Most of the plywood output produced for manufacturing tea chests is sold out to the offices of tea companies at Calcutta, though the same are ultimately meant for onward transmission to North Bengal, where the tea gardens are located.

(e) Major Constrants

For all groups of industries 'shortage of fund' is the most constraining factor. Then comes to the constraint of shortage of space. Lack of availability of raw material is the third major constraint. Lack of machinery is fourth ranking. Problems of storing of timber logs and drying up of veneers have created the problems of shortage of space.

It is also noticed that the share of export in the total value of output is insignificant. This is because that exportable quality of products is producible only with sophisticated machineries which most of the units do not have. Only a very few of the large units having such machineries export a small fraction of their total output.

E. The Clay Modelling Industry[f]

The clay modellers community of Kumartuli is famous for their doll making and clay modeling small industrial occupation. The age-old economically depressed and handicapped clay-modellers community mostly concentrated at Kumartuli area is to be promoted in their employment magnitudes in their traditional clay modeling occupation. Institutional finance has a great role to play so as to remove the economic and some of the essential infrastructural constraints of the community.

The clay modellers' families are grouped in a small area of nearby five acres span within ward no. 9 and little in ward no. 8 and the total number of units would be around 150.

In our analysis, 90-clay modeler's families have been incorporated. But nearly 60 families remain absent during the survey period. It was reported by the clay modelers that they are seasonal migrants to occupy their workspace and in off seasons they move away to their base of origin. Most of them belong to Krishna Nagar and Santipur in the district of Nadia.

All these units have a dominance over the clay modeling operation whose extent of coverage is nearly 95% on the totality of production and market as far as Kumartuli is concerned. There are five complementary sola craft units.

TABLE 1.7

Distribution of Clay Modellers by Age Group

Age	*Male*	*Female*	*Total*	*%age of Total*
Below 5	10	16	26	4.65
5-14	78	64	142	25.40
15-59	197	149	346	61.90
60 and above	25	19	44	7.87
Age no stated	1	—	.18	
Total	311	248	559	100.00

This population consists of: student population 149; working population 269; other working and minor dependents 141.

TABLE 1.8

Classification of Clay Modellers

	Adult		*Minor*		*Skilled*		*Unskilled*	
Type	*Male*	*Female*	*Male*	*Female*	*Male*	*Female*	*Male*	*Female*
Family Workers	175	10	30	54	170	52	35	12
Hired workers	268	—	40	—	234	—	74	—
Total	443	10	70	54	404	52	109	12

It may be observed from the above table, adult family workers (15-59) is 185 and the labour force in this age group of the families accounted for 346. The work participation rate with said age group is worked out to be 53.47%.

In clay modeling operation 577 workers are employed, of which 269 members belong to the resident clay modelers families. And the rest, 308 are hired workers (hired by these families). The female participants in such clay modeling and doll making are few. By skill, we mean those who are competent to carry out all stages of works starting from modeling to finish with finer parts of art. Unskilled workers are mostly assisting in the preparation of base materials and assembling them.

The five sola craft units run their production and business side by side with the doll making units in the Kumartuli pocket performing complementary activities to the doll making families in addition to the clay modeling engage themselves with some other industrial activities like clay craft and allied activities.

The numbers of work-shed units are approximately sixty. The doll makers bring along with them two hired labours on the average. So, the additional doll making workers during peak seasons rise up to nearly 180. This makes the doll making workers to figure 757.

The activities of the clay modelers are not very diverse and their off season activities have not yet been explored properly.

(a) Labour

Division of labour in clay modeling is not clearly visible except skilled and unskilled. They involve themselves from start to finish through different stages of activities. This is, as they remarked, necessary and helpful in exploring specific skill in making doll with specific design demanded by parties.

About all the people of the clay modeler's community live in very congested work-cum-living sheds, which are mostly old, dilapidated with Kacha floor and walls intertwined with bamboo sticks. Only three units have pucca structures with one story building. Some of the clay modelers have constructed sub floors and use them as their store space and sometimes for workspace too. With bent head amongst crowded dolls they exercise their artistic skill in giving shape to the dolls. They need some space to stand straight and to observe from a little distance to beautify the dolls in all respect up to their satisfaction. Some of the units have more than one work shed. The environmental condition is void of any architectural sense though colourful dolls are produced within this environment. The entire area is congested having very narrow lanes linking the work sheds from where the customers somehow bring out their selected dolls to the nearby wider road.

All the sheds of the clay modeling communities are on rental basis. The entire area was previously held by Zamindars. The area is now fragmented and owned by the heirs to whom all the rents and taxes are paid by the community.

(b) Raw Materials

Raw material used in doll making are—(1) Coarse materials – clay and timber, bamboo, hay, jute, wires etc. (2) Finer materials-paints, solasaj, clothes, jaries etc. It is estimated that four thousand cart loads (Thela) of clay are needed annually by them costing to Rs. 2 lakhs. There are about five clay traders who supply the clay to the doll makers at their location. The traders import their clay from Ganga-bed of Uluberia and even from near Diamond Harbour.

But all other material as such timber, bamboo, jute, wires etc. are collected by the producers from the markets, located at Maniktala and Barabazar. The prevailing practice of purchasing the inputs like clay and finer components like cloth, jaries etc. are largely on credit. The clay suppliers supply the desired type of clay to the location at the rate of Rs.50/- per thela, which help the modeling communities to a large extent but for this, they have to sacrifice some excess dues. The Barabazar traders take advantages in the seasonal demand market of some specific commodities, say for a cloth or jaries which doll makers need to meet ordered supply. They make some artificial scarcity on the specific commodity concerned for which doll producers are to sacrifice a lot. Thus, expect for bulk materials, the market of other material is subject to such fluctuation. The doll makers are thus handicapped by the prevailing situation.

(c) Production of Dolls

The artisans of Kumartuli have concentrated their skill mainly on doll making. But doll making has seasonality, which is connected with the seasonality of worshipping goddesses by the Hindus. However, from the doll maker's point of view, the following seasons have been clearly identified:

1. Durga Season

The Durga season is the most dominant, which include production of Durga, Kali, Ganesh, Viswakarma, Kartik, Lakshmi and Jagaddhatri. Production season starts approximately from April and continues to October, covering nearly seven months. Of course, the large-scale producers who can mobilise large capital and afford ample store place undertake the full seasons activities. The mechanism they follow is, from the beginning of April they start producing Lakshmi, Kali and send them to store space before giving final touch. This takes nearly three to four months after which the artisans take up concentration on producing Durga images on the already vacated workspace. Small producers including migrant producers cannot engage themselves for such longer duration because of many constraints i.e. constraints of store place, work space and capital. For them, this season is limited within three to four months.

2. Saraswati Season

Saraswati season is lone with Saraswati images only. The production season lasts for nearly two months and starts from around mid December. Therefore, for mid to high earners of artisan community the work period spread over nine months. Whereas for mid to low earners, it is limited to five or six months. For seasonal visitors this period is still less. Thus, for low to mid earners group whose percentage is nearly 31% find hard days by being thrown out of employment for nearly five to six months.

(d) Capital

In clay modeling industries fixed capital involved is comparatively insignificant. No machinery is involved in the process: only dices, brushes, trays constitute the magnitude of fixed capital. It is found that Durga season bears a ratio over Saraswati season at nearly 4:1, so far working capital is considered. During Durga season, nearly 75% of the working capital remains blocked for five to six months until the puja starts or ends. But for Saraswati season, it is blocked for two months only. However, capital is mainly obtained from own source and private loan at an exorbitant rate of interest from the Mahajans of Barabazar.

(e) Earning

A family can earn a profit of Rs. 3000/- p.a., on which they are to depend on an average, the members earn Rs. 285/- p.m., from clay modeling operation. On this earning their average family size of six members are to depend. It has also been observed that there is inequality of share of income as 31.10% of the poorer family enjoys only 12.6% of the income while 54.43% of the poorer family enjoys 31.81% of income. The disparity is, however, not too wide for the proportion of very upper class people as well as very poorer class people are comparatively small and nearly equal.

(f) Marketing

Most of the dolls are sold out from the production location. The owner-producer tackles all the transaction directly with customers. There is no area enmarked for public display, so that the customers could have exercised their choices. But the producers try to display their dolls on the roadsides to attract the customers. Kumartuli doll makers group have their established dominance in the Durga season over the Calcutta market. The market during Durga season is more or less assured for the Kumartuli artisan community. The market has been gradually spreading beyond the boundary of West Bengal. Some sales have been identified which had access to Bihar, Nepal, Assam and even export to UK Italy and USA in recent past.

But during Saraswati season, the Kumartuli image-makers are facing some troubles in market clearances, for which their losses during this season have been increasing over years. The reasons are (1) The worshippers are under different economic pressure for which they cannot offer much for dolls; (2) The sanctity and gravity of worshipping goddesses has at least partially deteriorated. People are more prone to external decoration with light, pandals rather than quality of dolls; (3) The production of Saraswati image have been spread in different zones within CMDA zone – so zonal worshippers meet their demand by the local supply; (4) Image makers from outside Kumartuli area import their dolls by road transport and display them in the road side in and around Kumartuli zones. The customers under the psychological satisfaction that they are purchasing the renowned Kumartuli dolls purchase the outside dolls with low bid. So the market of Kumartuli dolls is sometimes affected.

CONCLUSION

After reviewing some of the major small-scale industries based in Calcutta, it can be realised that these industries have a good resemblance with the informal sector criteria. All of these industries are, more or less, characterised by (i) reliance on domestic resources; (ii) family ownership; (iii) small-scale of operation; (iv) labour intensity and adapted technology; (v) skills acquired outside the formal school system; (vi) unregulated and competitive markets which are all the features of informal sector as laid down by the ILO. Besides, one could also enumerate such features as seasonality in production level and consequently in employment level.

In addition, another striking fact is, out of the five industries we have discussed in this chapter, the tailoring industry of Garden Reach and the timber and plywood industry of Ultadanga are remarkable in a sense that the former has a historical background while the latter has been established in that particular area due to its geographical advantage.

However, other than these industries, there are hosiery industries of Shobha Bazar in Central Calcutta, paper packet industry of Muraripukur in east Calcutta, leather goods industry of Park Circus in southeast Calcutta etc. If these industries can also be surveyed, there is every possibility of disclosure of such facts, which might enrich the informal sector concept.

REFERENCES

(a) It indicates 'earthen rampart'.

(b) Mongola haat: This haat was initiated by a Hindu Zamindar who wanted to provide the local tailoring industry with a marketing outlet so as to counter the Manchester fabrics which threatened to completely ruin the indigenous textile industry and actually did to a great extent. The haat was a calculated move aimed at strengthening the 'swadeshi' cloth.

(c) Data for this part are gathered from (i) 'A project report on small tanners and ancillary groups of Eastern Calcutta' by Kalikata bustee pragati sangha in 1977 and (ii) 'A scheme for resettlement of small tanners', by j.Basu Roy Chowdhury and Dr.T.H.Thomas.

(d) Figures quoted by Dr. Sudhendu Mukherhjee in his study: 'Informal Sector': the only hope of the urban poor in a metropolis' Mimeographed document.

(e) This part of our work is based on the study report, no: 48, June '77: Economic and Social Support Programme Cell. Director of planning, CMDA, June '77.

(f) Compiled from Report no: 47. June '77, Director of planning, CMDA, June '77.

NOTES

1. Linking factors for deriving the consumer price index on base 1981-1982=100 from 1990-1991=100 based series is 1.811 and between 1990-1991=100 and 2001-2002=100 is 2.813 [Source: National Accounts Statistics, Central Statistics Organisation]

2. Industrial wage index for the urban workers of the small-scale units, considering the base year 1981-1982=100 comes to 362.8 in 2001-2002. [Source: Indian Labour Statistics, Ministry of Labour, Govt. of India]

3. The minimum wage legislation, as it stands now, in the state of West Bengal, Is as follow: Unskilled workers: 41.08; semiskilled workers: 43.17 and skilled workers: 47.21 [Source: Bureau of Applied Economics & Statistics, Govt. of WB, 2001-2002]

3

Highlighting Informal Slum Industries Around Calcutta

Slum industries, being a major part of the informal sector, have been highlighted in this chapter. For case study, we have selected Pilkhana slum in the district of Howrah, which is adjacent to Calcutta. Our survey results confirm that the small and tiny units, operating in Pilkhana slum, undeniably have the characteristics of the informal sector. In addition, the industries surveyed, can be divided into three categories according to their productivity and income. We have also noted two basic conditions, which are responsible for the survival and growth of the informal sector units of Pilkhana slum. To conclude with, our opinion is fairly lucid: the role-played by the informal sector in terms of income and employment cannot be substituted in the metropolitan economy. It is, therefore, necessary to implement specific policies towards the informal sector, which should include all essential aspects like production, employment, investment, amelioration of working conditions and wages etc.

Preamble

In '71, out of a total population in Calcutta metropolitan district of 83,30,000, two and a half million people were living in slums (30% of the total population). Proportion of slum dwellers in Calcutta city is still higher as 12,50,000, out of 29,27,000 (43%) live in slums[a]. Slums, not only areas where an extremely dense population lives but also concentrate an intense economic activity, notably industrial as most informal sector units are located there.

A survey conducted on behalf of CMDA by a team of consultants[(b)] on a group of bustees in north Calcutta enumerated 1934 units, most of them of family type, employing 4,803 people (2.48 per unit on average) with an average investment of Rs. 7,549/- per unit. Breaking down these units into industrial groups shows a high concentration in tailoring and hosiery industries, followed by light engineering, wood and electrical industries. Constraints of lack of capital, space, electricity, raw materials and market are quoted by respondents as being the most difficult (respectively by 8,44,01,810 and 7% of them). As far as capital is concerned, initial finance was mainly invested out of the entrepreneur's own funds but the proportion of non-institutional loan sources is predominant: four fifths of borrowings come from such sources. Problems relating to raw materials are connected with lack of capital, as unit owners, specially tailors, have to depend on middlemen who supply raw materials and buy finished products while paying to the unit nominal labour charges. Lastly, sale of quite a few products, considered to be of insufficient quality for marketing in organised networks, is done by hawkers who sell them on foothpaths: such products, manufactured by informal sector workers are sold to consumers of the same sector who look for low prices and for whom quality is immaterial. Slum industries show similar features as far as social aspects are concerned: long working hours, bad working conditions and extremely low wages, particularly for women and children who are many in these industries, without taking into account the total lack of job security. Bela Banerjee[c] in an article on the role of women in Calcutta's informal sector, lists the main industries where women compose a cheap, docile and non-organised workforce; There are: rubber products, ampoule, sandals and leather goods, paper bags, tailoring and waste recycling. In 'wild' establishments located in narrow lanes or by-lanes, work is irregular and depends on seasonal market fluctuations or on supply of raw materials. The wages of women surveyed do not go beyond Rs. 5/- per day in the best cases; average would be around Rs. 40/- to Rs. 50/- per month. Some of these establishments are linked with large companies which farm out components or parts for manufacture. Such parts and components are bought from these units at a very low price (allowed by low wages), assembled and sold by the 'parent' company under its own brand with a substantial profit margin. Such is the case of electrical components, manufactured in small units and sold to multinational companies who would spend twice or thrice as much of money if they were to be produced by them. Such subcontracting linkage based on exploitation of labour, specially female, enable formal sector units to be competitive on international markets and to remunerate the invested capital. Dr. S. Mukherjee [d] enumerates amongst other industries with large employment in Calcutta slums: tobacco and biri industries, chemical industries, soap manufacturing and printing presses.

The result of a survey conducted in Pilkhana slum will complement these general aspects of informal sector industries through the availability of primary data.

Results of a Survey on Slum Industries in Pilkhana, Howrah

Pilkhana is a slum of 70,000 inhabitants located in the heart of Howrah, the industrial twin-city of Calcutta. It was selected for a survey meant to study the working conditions of small-scale industries belonging to the informal sector of the metropolitan economy for the following reasons:

— Geographically, the slum is well demarcated: roughly, it is a square with an area of less than one square kilometer.

— Pilkhana, a slum which was formed more than 40 years ago, is a 'residential' area as well as a place where intense economic activity, industrial and tertiary, takes place. In the latter sector many small shopkeepers and vendors are to be found. Industries are mostly engineering workshops, which confirms the preeminence Howrah has gained in this regard.

— To the eyes of an outsider, these industries show straight off characteristics of the informal sector: small size, restricted space, and small number of machines, simple technology.

— Lastly, the author of the survey had many contacts [e] in Pilkhana who made it easier for him to have access to the unit owners.

The survey was carried out during two months from Nov. '88 to Jan. '89. It covered 60 randomly selected industries. Such a sample may be considered as sufficient (if one takes into account the time factor) to allow one to observe trends and make an in-depth study of a small part of the informal sector industrial units. The main hurdle of the survey (as of any survey on non-organised sector) was the extreme difficulty of getting reliable figures, for two major reasons:

The reluctance of many unit owners to disclose the invested capital, turnover, and value added and profit, for fear of income tax. The assurance given that only the university will use the figures does not quell the apprehensions.

The fact that a large number of unit owners do not know the figures: out of 60 owners, 18 only keep accounts (30%).

It is, therefore, necessary to be cautious in dealing with the data gathered, as one has to include the margin of error with which the interviewers enunciate them, voluntarily or involuntarily. One has tried to cross-examine the figures, but error cannot be totally eliminated.

(A) Number and Type of Units Surveyed

Out of 60 units, 7 had to be excluded from the tabulation: in one case, the unit had no worker at the time of the survey and had been closed for 2 years. It was about to re-open in a different line. Another case was of the 'subsidiary' of a unit already surveyed. In the 5 other cases, the figures quoted were contradictory and incoherent. The table below shows the distribution of the 53 units by industrial group.[f]

Light engineering industries are predominant, as they constitute 2/3rd of the sample. The largest numbers of machines are hand or ball presses, followed by polishing, grinding and shaping machines, as well as by lathes. In chemical industries quite a few units make plastic ball pens with injection machines. 21 units (40%) are without power and have to be content with hand tools. 25 units produce intermediate goods and 28 units produce final products.

TABLE 1.9

Distribution of the Units by Industrial Group

Engineering Industries	35	Pen Parts: 5; Domestic utensils: 5; Radio Parts: 2; Air Conditioner parts: 1; Umbrella Rings: 1; Washers: 6; links, clips: 3; Steel trunks: 3; Various Parts: 5; Galvanization: 1; Polishing: 1; Anodizing: 1; Electroplating: 1.
Chemical Industries	9	Ball stens: 5; Caps: 1; Battery Covers: 2; Sandals: 1
Textile Industries	4	Thread winding: 1; Bags, Collars: 2; Sari Printing: 1
Wood Industries	2	Photo Frames: 1; Loud Speaker frames: 1.
Ceramic Industries	2	Earthen teacups: 2.
Food Industries	1	Bakery; 1.
Total	53	

(B) Main Characteristics

47 units are proprietorships and only 6(11%) are partnerships. No unit is a private limited co., or a co-operative. Most of the units are recent: 2/3rd were started less than 5 years ago, as shown in the table:

TABLE 1.10

Age of Surveyed Units

	Less than One Year	*One Year Three Years*	*Three Years Five Years*	*Five Years– Ten Years*	*More than Ten Years*	*Total*
No. of Units	13	18	4	10	8	53
Per cent	25	34	7	19	15	100

One quarter of the units were started in the year preceeding the date of the survey, which illustrates the vitality of the informal sector. The creation of new units goes together with closure of non-viable units: 2 owners said they had to close the units they were owning and the list of industries which applied for loans shows at least 2 units closed after applying for the same. Yet the number of new units is by far larger than that of closed units.

Only 11 units (20%) are registered as small-scale industries and one under the Factories Act. 2 owners mentioned that they would register themselves as S.S.I. Though 23 owners are aware of the facilities reserved for S.S.I., 6 only tried, but in vain, to obtain them. Thus, the gap between the policy in favour of small-scale industries and its actual implementation in the informal sector is confirmed. All units rely on themselves to survive and possibly, grow in a very competitive market. Even if nearly half the unit owners assert that they know there is a government policy supposed to help them, they think that it will not be possible for them to get the facilities planned on paper. Then, whereas the usual measures of promoting small-scale industries have not touched Pilkhana, a programme well adjusted to the needs of the informal sector units is more likely to succeed. 26 units out of 53 (one out of two) have applied for a loan, but so far only 3 have got it.

23 units (47%) work in workshop having an area less than 10 metre squares. In all 9 units out of 10 have to be content with workshops of less than 50 metre square, as shown below:

TABLE 1.11

Workshop Area of the Surveyed Units

	Less than 10 metre Square	*10 to 20 metre Square*	*20 to 50 metre Square*	*50 to 100 metre Square*	*More than 100 metre Square*	*Total*
No. of Units	23	16	8	4	2	53
Per cent	43	30	15	8	4	100

The table illustrates the unimaginable concentration of space and density in a bustee like Pilkhana and the adjustments made by the unit owners to these geographic and human realities. Similarly, 23 workshops (43%) are used only for industry, 19(36%) mainly for industry and 11 (20%) both for industry and residence.

In 39 units (73%) work is continuous throughout the year whereas 12 units (23%) work only 6 to 9 months and 2 units (4%) work even less than 6 months in a year. As one will see, lack of capital is the main reason for the under utilisation of installed capacities. Moreover, all units operate only one shift per day.

(C) Employment

The 53 units of the survey give employment to 329 persons, without counting 8 partners or owners who work occasionally. Each unit employs 6.2 persons, which is high for informal sector units [(g)]. 43% units have 5 workers or less, 49% from 5 to 9 and 8% only more than 10 workers. The table shows the employment distribution:

Hired workers (including Supervisors and Accountants) account for more than 3/4th of employment. Amongst them, only 13 women are to be found (4% of total employment). The work force includes 19 children although law prohibits employment of children below 14 years. Amongst children, one is a non-paid apprentice, one is an unpaid family member and if 4 are paid the same rate as adult workers, the remaining 13 have very low wages: the average wage of the 17 paid children amounts to Rs. 30/ - per week, whereas all workers get an average Rs. 51/- per week approximately.

TABLE 1.12

Distribution of Employment of Surveyed Units

	Appren-tices	*Unpaid Family members*	*Hired Workers*	*Supervisors Accountant*	*Owners*	*Total*
No. of labour	3	29	241	9	47	329
Per cent	1	9	73	3	14	100

The questionnaire had one question on workers' qualification. The respondent was asked to distinguish between skilled and unskilled workers. It turns to be that such a distinction is not relevant. Most of the jobs ate repetitive, monotonous and non-skilled. They require only a short on-the-job training. Only the owners can be considered as skilled as they know a particular job and made it basis of their industries. In a few cases, the respondent says he has amongst his workers a 'mistri' able to supervise the work in his absence.

Similarly, it is not possible to have a clear-cut separation between permanent and temporary employees. Informal sector units are characterised by a complete lack of job security : workers, be they old or new, have to make themselves adjust to the conditions dictated by the market on the other hand, though it was not possible to quantify it, labour turnover is quite high.

Average wages, calculated on 242 paid workers (including one paid apprentice) amount to Rs. 50.75 per week (most workers get their wage once a week). The 5 supervisors who have much higher wages and the 4 accountants, who all work part time, have been excluded from the calculation.

TABLE 1.13

Distribution of Surveyed Workers by Size of Weekly Wages (In Rupees)

	Less than 24	*24-35*	*36-47*	*48-59*	*60-71*	*72-89*	*90-119*	*More than 120*	*Total*
No. of Workers	18	45	28	65	42	19	15	10	242
Per cent	7	19	12	27	17	8	6	4	100

38% of the workers get less than Rs. 48/- per week and 82% of them less than Rs. 72/-. For comparison sake, the minimum wages as fixed by the government of West Bengal was around Rs. 8/- per day in '81 (Rs. 48/- for a 6 day week); in organised industries, wages of the least qualified workers are around Rs. 350/- per month (Rs. 87.50 per week), an amount which more than three quarters of the surveyed workers do not reach.

Once again, the low level of wages must be stressed[h]. Knowing the average weekly wages of a worker in small Pilkhana industry, it is possible to estimate the average family income per capita form data of a survey conducted in '79 in an area more or less identical to Pilkhana[i]. According to this survey, there was an average of 1.42 earners per family, each family have 3.15 members. Assuming that the earners have the same wage as the workers of Pilkhana slum industries the per capita monthly income comes to Rs. 91.51 at per with poverty line of Rs. 90.80 in Nov.'88[j]. In 60% of the units, wages are based on piece-rates. In 28% of cases, wages ate calculated according to time and 4% of the units combine both systems, 4 uints have no hired workers, the gross surplus being shared between the owners and the family members. All units report working hours from 8 to 17 hours, i.e. to say minimum 48 hours per week (Saturday full day and one hour lunch or tea-break per day). All units are closed on Sundays. As a matter of fact, timings as reported by respondents are never sticked to : they vary according to production needs and orders and for units which use power, to the daily power cuts. Frequent power cut forces workers to remain idle during 'official' working hours and to make up for the loss of production by working overtime late at night when there is power. Less than 10% of their owners report overtime payment; 9 only (17%) pay a bonus to their worker whereas it is compulsory in organised sector industries.

Of the employees 69% reside in Pilkhana itself, 24% in Howrah and only 7% outside. The percentage of persons residing near their working place is even higher as 89% live in Pilkhana where most of them were born (those who were not born in Pilkhana have been staying for more than 15 years). The fact that the larger part of workers and owners were born and live in Pilkhana[k] demonstrates that it is a relatively old settlement with an almost total lack of recent immigration. Only 13 workers state that they have settled down recently and temporarily in Pilkhana : 6 come from West Bengal's rural areas and 7 from other states of eastern India (4 from Orissa, 3 from Bihar).

Out of 270 employees for whom the data is available[l], 60 (22%) are illiterate, 121 (45%) have not gone beyond primary school and 73 (27%) went to secondary school but without completing their studies. 16 only (6%) passed their school final; amongst them the supervisors, accountants and mistris are to be found. As expected the educational level of unit-owners is higher than their employees : 5% are illiterate, 29% did not go beyond primary studies, 35% attended secondary school and 31% completed secondary school. Amongst the latter some went to university (less than 10%).

The last question was related to religion. 66% of employees and 82% of owners are Muslims, which were to be expected in a predominantly Muslim slum (70% of total population are muslim).

(D) Invested Capital, Turnover and Value Added

Fixed capital only has been estimated i.e. the value of machines, tools and implement used in the production process.[(m)] it was decided not to assess working capital because of the difficulty of being precise about this notion and the inability of most entrepreneurs to answer the question relating to it. In all fixed capital for the 53 units of the survey amounts to Rs. 7,01,375/-, i.e. to say an average of Rs. 13,233/- per unit. Such an average encompasses wide variations : as shown in the table below, the largest number of units 16 (30%) are in the capital size of Rs. 1,000/- — Rs. 4,999/-, whereas 12 units (23%) are in the size of Rs. 5,000/- - Rs. 9,999/- and 10 (19%) in Rs. 10,000/ - - Rs. 24,999/-. There is a correlation between the amount of fixed capital and the employment of the units.

Yet, if a small fixed capital allows for employment of a few people at the other end of the scale a high amount of fixed capital (above Rs. 25,000/-) does not necessarily mean high employment.

TABLE 1.14

Distribution of Surveyed Units by Capital and Employment Size

Capital : (in Rs.)	*Less than 1,000*	*1000- 4,999*	*5000- 9,999*	*10,000– 24,999*	*25,000– 49,999*	*More than 50,000*	*Total*
Employment							
Less than 3	4	3	—	—	—	—	7
4-5	1	6	6	1	2	—	16
6-7	1	7	4	6	—	1	19
8-9	1	—	2	—	2	2	7
10-12	—	—	—	1	1	—	2
13-15	—	—	—	1	—	—	1
More than 15	—	—	—	1	—	—	1
Total	7	16	12	10	5	3	53

Fixed capital per worker amounts to Rs. 2,132/- which is very little in relation to the capital required to employ one person in the organised sector. This statement remain true even if one takes into account a probable under estimation of the fixed capital, due to the owners' fear of income tax. 1/3rd of the units have only second hand machines, 27% new machines and 27% both new and second hand. In one unit the owner made his machines himself, whereas 5 units (10%) have no proper machines but only a few hand tools. Capital-low and labour intensive technology as utilised by these small-scale industries is particularly relevant in a country where capital is scarce and labour abundant.

One question was related to the origin of the capital invested in the units; in more than half of the units (52%), the owner invested his own funds and in 23% of the units capital was inherited. The remaining units (1/4th) combine various loans from friends and relatives (without interest except in one unit) alongwith self owned and inherited funds. Only one respondent reports a loan from a money lender at the interest rate of 7% per month.

The monthly turnover of the 49 units for which figures are available amounts to Rs. 5,80,110/- or an average of Rs. 11,838/- per unit. Nearly 39% of the units are in the size of Rs. 10,000/- to Rs. 24,999/- and 36% in Rs. 1,000/ - to Rs. 4,999/- as shown in the table below :

TABLE 1.15

Distribution of Surveyed Units by Capital and Turnover Size

Capital : (in Rs.)	*Less than 1,000*	*1000-4,999*	*5000-9,999*	*10,000–24,999*	*25,000–49,999*	*More than 50,000*	*Total*
Turnover (in Rs.)							
Less than 1,000	2	—	—	—	—	—	2
1,000–4,999	4	10	2	2	—	—	18
5,000–9,999	—	2	—	2	1	—	5
10,000–24,999	1	4	7	2	2	3	19
25,000–49,999	—	—	—	2	2	—	4
More than 50,000	—	—	1	—	—	—	1
Total	7	16	10	8	5	3	49

Out of 49 units, 6 do job work : they transform raw materials that do not belong to them (Sari printing, polishing, thread winding etc.). Thus a high amount of capital sometimes goes along with a small turnover as the latter does not include the cost of raw materials.

TABLE 1.16

Distribution of Surveyed Units by Capital and Value Added Size

Capital : (in Rs.)	*Less than 1,000*	*1000-4,999*	*5000-9,999*	*10,000–24,999*	*25,000–49,999*	*More than 50,000*	*Total*
Value Added (in Rs.)							
Less than 500	3	2	—	—	—	—	5
500 – 999	1	2	—	—	—	—	3
1,000 – 2,499	1	9	6	1	—	—	17
2,500 – 4,999	—	2	4	3	5	—	14
Above 5,000	—	—	—	1	—	2	3
Total	5	15	10	5	5	2	42

Value added by production was available for only 42 units. Monthly value added amounts to Rs. 1,01,510/- or Rs. 2,417/- per unit (Rs. 383/- per worker). Value added per worker per year amounts to Rs. 4,596/- a figure that is much lower than the one mentioned in the Ahmedabad survey quoted above (where value added per worker per year amounts to Rs. 29,728/-). Value added constitutes 19.53% of turnover of the 42 units. The gross surplus amounts to Rs. 55,045/- (Rs. 1,311/- per units) which includes the remuneration of the family labour and of the owner himself, depreciation of equipment and remuneration of invested capital. Total value added is thus divided into two nearly equal parts : 54% remunerate capital and labour brought by the owner and his family and 46% hired labour. If one deducts from the surplus accruing to the owner the imputed wages of family labour (at the same rate as calculated above)[(n)] monthly income per unit comes to Rs. 1,190/- or 5.41 times as much as average labour wages. This average is a satisfactory income when compared to invested capital and prevailing low wages but it hides wide differences between units with a low capital in which income of the owner hardly exceeds the wages of the hired labour and other units with a higher capital and a substantial income. Correlation between value added and fixed capital is to be underlined as shown in the above table.

Labour productivity increases proportionally to fixed capital : whereas monthly value added per worker is Rs. 176/- for units with a capital below Rs. 1,000/-, it reaches to Rs. 319/-, Rs. 419/-, Rs. 490/- and Rs. 887/- for units with a capital size of Rs. 1,000/- - Rs. 4,999/-, Rs. 5,000/- - Rs. 9,999/-, Rs. 25,000/- — Rs. 49,999/- and more than Rs. 50,000/- respectively. The ratio of annual value added to fixed capital of the 42 units considered comes to 2.22 : a unit of fixed capital generates every year 2.22 units of value added. Such an average has to be considered with cautiousness as it encompasses wide variation as well as limitations in the reliability of the data collected.

(E) Working of the Unit and Owners' Opinion

61% of the units sell their products to wholesalers of Calcutta's markets, specially Barabazar, 25% to manufactures, 8% to both and 6% to retailers. Only 2 units sell outside Calcutta. Out of 53 units, 6 only are paid cash, whereas 78% deliver their goods on credit and 11% combined both systems. The duration of credit in 85% of the units is below one month, as shown Table 1.17.

Only one unit complains about delays in getting payments. 8 others report some irregularity or occasional delays. 83% of the units do not face any difficulty in this respect whatsoever. The problem of delayed payments, often mentioned as a major constraint of small-scale units, does not arise in Pilkhana.

TABLE 1.17

Duration of Credit Given by Surveyed Units to Their Buyers

	Less than 1 week	*1 week-15 days*	*15 days-1 month*	*1 month-2 months*	*2 months-3 months*	*Total*
No. of units	6	13	21	4	3	47
Per cent	13	27	45	9	6	100

56% of the industries get their raw materials from wholesalers, 25% from manufacturers, 8% from retailers and 11% form the three of them. Raw materials are supplied in 65% of the cases against cash payment and on credit in 17%; 18%; of the units have both. Thus, the respondents receive from their suppliers less credit than what they allow to their client and duration of credit received is lower than credit allowed. The overall indebtedness of the small-scale units with a low capital base worsens their difficulties relating to lack of capital.

Answers to the question on the constraints the owners have to face, reflect their own opinion on the working and environment of their units. 15 owners did not answer. The table shows how many times one particular constraint was reported by the 38 left:

TABLE 1.18

Main Constraints Reported by United-Owners

Constraints	*No. of times it is reported*
Lack of capital	28
Lack of power	7
Lack of orders	6
Lack if skilled labour	2
Difficulties in getting raw materials	1

Lack of capital is for the most mentioned constraint being cited by 3/4th of the owners who answered. Perennial lack of funds, not for expansion of the units but specially for working capital needs, is the main reason, more than lack of orders quoted only 6 times for the under utilisation of installed capacities which is shown specifically, as mentioned earlier, by the lack of continuous work throughout the year of 23% of the units. Very few owner report market constraint and this is in accordance with answers to another question on demand: more than 4/5th of the owners who answered gave the opinion that demand for their products was good. Surprisingly enough, only 7 owners report power cuts; spherically when it has become a daily feature to which small-scale units have had to adjust (thanks to the flexibility of working hours imposed on labour). The difficulty 'lack of skilled labour' is amazing in Pilkhana where industrial units do a non-specialised job and there is an abundant manpower that have had basic on-the-job training in successive workshops. The fact that the constraint of supply of raw materials is mentioned only once confirms the overall availability of all inputs in Calcutta even if prices of commodities such as iron and steel on the 'free market' exceed by far the rates fixed by government.

Resorting to bank loans is seen as the main way of avoiding lack of capital. No respondent had a bank loan at the time of the survey, expect 3 who had just received in the few months preceding it a CMDA sponsored loan. Besides this, 3 units owners had taken loans from other sources: one from friends and relatives with an interest rate of 10% p.a. and 2 from money lenders with a rate of 5% and 7% per month. Generally speaking, Pilkhana's informal sector units manage with their own resources without resorting to external finances, be it from institutional or non-institutional sources. Moneylenders make huge profits on loans for consumption but not any loans for production, which are almost non-existent.

The quasi-absence of external finance does not mean that respondents did not try to get it. 6 owners tried to take advantage of the facilities made available by government to small-scale units : 5 applied for loans and 1 for raw materials at controlled rates. In 4 cases applicants have given up : the 2 others had not yet got the facilities applied for, this shows clearly that a promotion programme not adjusted specifically to the needs of informal sector units is most likely not to reach the targeted beneficiaries. CMDA's programme meets these requirements and has meet with some amount of success in Pilkhana. Thanks to the initiative taken by a local committee[o]. Out of 53 units surveyed, 26 had applied for a loan and 3 had already been sanctioned and disbursed a loan. Yet this programme is not free of the usual bureaucratic hurdles: some loan applications have been pending for more than 2 years and long time gaps elapse between the sanction and the disbursement of a loan 44% of applicants want to utilize the loan to meet their working capital needs, 20% to acquire new machines and 36% for both. 15 units (for which data are available) have applied for loans totalling Rs. 3,01,000/- (Rs. 20,066/ - per unit on a average) and plan to hire 54 more workers. Capital (fixed and working) required to employ one additional worker comes to Rs : 5,574/-. This figure is consistent with the average amount of fixed capital invested per unit. It corroborates the low capital per worker required in informal sector industries.

(F) Some Notable Facts

As written earlier average figures hide wide variation between units. All undeniably have the characteristics of the informal sector that the survey results confirm : low capital and high labour intensity, low wages, owners' income enabling them to be better off than his workers but insufficient for re-investment in the unit which is shown in the perennial dearth of capital reported by the majority of owners. Some case studies shall complement these overall trends and underline the diversity of the situations in which Pilkhana's small-scale units find themselves.

One end of the spectrum is represented by the 2 ceramic units and by the rubber-sandal making unit. In these 3 cases, invested capital and income are extremely low (less than Rs. 200/- and Rs. 250/- p.m. respectively). There is no hired worker but only family labour. These extreme cases are more properly to be considered as handicraft rather than as industrial units : activity is based on a very simple traditional technology and none of these units use machines. The sandal making unit, moreover, an instance (found in 2 more cases during the survey) of mixing business and family funds : the entrepreneur who is a full time employee of a company at Calcutta, started his unit so as to give employment and income to both of his unemployed brothers. But he had to take money from the working capital so as to finance his sister's wedding. The unit had then to close for several months.

Another unit manufactures simple cycle parts and clips: though the invest capital is around Rs. 25,000/-, the unit runs at a loss; It's owner works in the afternoon shift of a factory and a part of his wages is invested in his unit, the turnover of which does not exceed Rs. 1,000/- p.m. and which has only unpaid family member.

A unit, manufacturing clips too, with a fixed capital of Rs. 4,500/- has a surplus of only Rs. 160/- p.m. only female workers work in this unit. 6 women earn less than Rs. 15/- per week. This is also an extreme example of extremely low capital and labour productivity.

Unit manufacturing steel trunks require a low fixed investment, as no machine is needed. One of the 3 such units under the survey, has a monthly turnover (checked in the books of accounts) of Rs. 2,333/- which leaves the owner a monthly surplus of Rs. 150/-, lower than the wages of his workers (Rs. 260/-). Besides, the unit is located in an open space and cannot run during the monsoon months.

Manufactures of pen parts and domestic aluminum utensils, as well as plastic ball-pens, is a line of products of which data are more or less similar to the average as calculated above " capital in the range of Rs. 5,000/- —Rs. 10,000/-, surplus between Rs. 500/- and Rs. 1,000/- per month.

At the other end of the spectrum, the cases of two successful industries may be quoted :

— The first one manufactures aluminum parts for air conditioners. It is one of the two units of the survey that sells its products outside Calcutta. Invested fixed capital is above Rs. 60,000/- and though the figure of surplus was not available, the 'asset' side of the balance-sheet showing 'bank' with Rs. 17,000/- and 'debtors' with Rs. 20,000/- is a sign of very substantial profits. The unit belongs to the wife of the entrepreneur who works as supervisor with a fixed salary of

Rs. 600/- p.m. Other workers get fixed wages of Rs. 150/- (2 workers) and Rs. 210/- (4 workers) p.m., lower than the average of Rs. 50.75 per week (Rs. 220/- p.m.) Then even in very profitable companies, market wages prevail whatever the productivity differences may be. The profit accrues to the owner only without any part of it being shared with the employees.

— The second one manufactures battery cell covers of automobiles. The entrepreneur has devised his own formula in bakelite for this product which is usually made in hard rubber. Though investment is relatively low (less than Rs. 500/-) a turnover of Rs. 87,000/- in '80, checked from the P & L A/C kept by the owner, left him with a surplus of Rs. 16,000/- (Rs 1,333/- p.m.). This is the only case of a unit that has developed its own product. In all other cases, the product is copied from units manufacturing a similar item or is a family tradition[p]. This may explain why Pilkhana concentrates the manufacture of only a few products[q].

Conclusions

The results of this survey allow one to delineate the contrasts of small-scale industries in Pilkhana. A break down of the industries surveyed into 3 categories make it possible to have a shaded perception of the whole, though limited, they constitute. The first category groups low productivity units, the income of which accruing to the owner, after deducting the imputed wages of family labour, is inferior or equal to the average wages: 15 units would fall into this category or 28%; The second one groups units the economic characteristic of which correspond more or less to the average: 24 units (46%) come into this category; Lastly, the third category groups units which have succeeded in one way or another: the owners' income exceeds Rs. 1,500/- p.m. This category has 14 units (26%). Thus, more than 2/3rd of the units surveyed enable their owners to draw a 'decent' income, inclusive of the remuneration of their labour and capital, even if it is much lower than incomes in the formal sector.

Two basic conditions explain the survival and development of informal sectors units, as well as it's capacity to provide employment to numerous non-skilled workers. The first one is the very low wages of hired labour (Rs. 220/- p.m. on an average) who have to accept long working hours and a complete lack of job security, as well as deplorable working conditions: small space, lack of safety[r], insufficient lighting. Formal and informal sectors are thus demarcated by a clear-cut separation. Whereas in the former the level of employment is fixed by a demand for labour at given wage rate. In the latter the abundance of the stock and flow of labour means that demand variables like productivity do not play any role in determining wages: they fix themselves at subsistence levels much lower than those of the organised sector. Second, these small units depend entirely on prices imposed by the market on which they do not exert the slightest control because of competition against one another, lack of specialisation and simplicity of techniques utilised. The predominant role of dealers-wholesalers in Calcutta has already been underlined: they not only dictate the selling price but also the prices at which informal sector units should buy their raw materials. The same statement applied to manufacturers with which quite a few units deal. Informal unit establishments cannot earn per unit of production the same income as in the formal sector.

Finally, informal sector units supply, a considerable number of low priced goods and provide jobs to people who, otherwise, would swell the ranks of unemployed. This kind of production and job creation is possible with a low capital raised through the owners' funds. But the working conditions of these units make them subservient to the formal sector of the metropolitan economy, be it organised industry or trade. The workers and owners of these units derive from them means of subsistence, which cannot be compared with the facilities, the formal sector employees get.

Besides, it remains that working conditions of informal sector units are detrimental to their workers. One has stressed the fact that even in cases of higher productivity, wages remain the same, which indicates a higher degree of workers exploitation particularly when value added. and capital invested per unit rise.

To sum up, the role-played by the informal sector in terms of employment and income cannot be substituted for in the metropolitan economy. Rather than to wait for the hypothetical advantages of an overall development policy to percolate down to the down trodden, it is necessary to conceive and implement specific policies towards the informal sector. Such policies should be justified in terms of production, employment and capital and should go along with regulations on the working conditions and wages of this sector.

REFERENCES

(a) Density in Calcutta's slums is 83,000 inhabitants per square kilometer as against 34,000 in Calcutta city.

(b) Team consultants Pvt. Ltd.: Socio-economic survey in bustees of Calcutta. Report 110 and 112, July '80.

(c) Bela Banerjee: "Women workers in the informal sector of industry in Calcutta" an article published in the Journal of All India Women's Association in September. '79.

(d) Dr. S. Mukherjee: "Informal sector: the only hope of the urban poor in a metropolis". Ibid.

(e) Thanks to Seva Sangh Samiti, a social welfare and development organisation which has been working in Pilkhana for the last 15 years in the field of health, education and improvement of the slum environment.

(f) Besides, in course of this survey, we have also paid proper heed to some other means of living of the inhabitants of Nandy Bagan, adjacent to Pilkhana slum. From a separate point of view, these have been analysed in chapter five.

(g) In a survey on Ahmedabad, informal sector industries average size is 3.28 per unit: c. T.S. Papola: Urban informal sector in a developing economy; Vikas Publishing House, '81.

(h) Figures of wages are much more reliable than other data and can be considered as depicting exactly labour working conditions, as they are not 'sensitive' data (unlike capital or profit) and are concrete figures which respondents know in all cases.

(i) Kalikata Bustee Pragati Sangh: Integrated Bustee Development Programme. Report of a survey in 10 selected micro-communities, '79. One of the micro-communities is Fakir Bagan, Salkia, a part of which is in Pilkhana; Socio-economic data were gathered on 1082 families of this area.

(j) Poverty line was defined in '60 as a per capita monthly income of Rs. 20/-. The consumer price index for industrial workers reached 454 in November '88 with '60: 100.

(k) Average age of employees is below 30 years and of owners below 35 years.

(l) 12 employees did not answer.

(m) Capital invested in land and building was not assessed; as only 28% of the units have their own buildings. For the 72% which rent their premises, average monthly rent is Rs. 84/-

(n) Each unit has on an average. 55 family workers. At the weekly rate of Rs. 50.75, which is the average wages of hired labour as shown above, the remuneration of a family worker comes to Rs. 121/- per month (a month has 26 working days).

(o) Pilkhana Bustee Improvement Committee: 2 members of this committee systematically visited Pilkhana's small-scale industries and helped the owners to fill-in the loan application form.

(p) For example, Steel trunks unit owners all of whom came from Allahabad where from they introduced the industry in Pilkhana.

(q) Specially pen parts, domestic utensils, steel trunks, washers and metallic clips, ball pens etc.

(r) Particularly in units using automatic lathes linked to an electric motor through belts, the breaking of which could have dreadful consequences.

4

The Organisation of Work in the Informal Sector*

This study enlightens the organisation of work among the scavengers on the Bantala Dumping Ground, in the city of Kolkata, India. They work for the large industrial consumers of recuperated materials without any direct relationship with them. They organise themselves at work in a special manner. There, too, exist different processes for executing the work, allotment of time among such processes and repeated buying and selling though in an uncommon way. They can be characterised as independent workers possessing a calm nature in general though occasionally cantankerous. They are solely concerned about protecting their right to work but not in a position to improve their working conditions due to the interaction of some barriers prevail in transit.

PREAMBLE

Since early '70's the unplanned sector of the third world metropolis has been reviewed critically by social scientists. This is evidenced by the voluminous literature

* For an abridged version of this portion of our work, please see: Chowdhury, Dr. Utpal [1995] "The Organisation of work in the informal sector" in *The Indian Economic Journal* [Bangalore, India], Oct.–Dec. 1995, Vol. 43, No. 2, pp. 110-121.

A complete view can be had from: Chowdhury, Dr. Utpal [1996] "Organisation of work in decadent modernism" in *The Uttaraadhunik* [Worthington, Ohio, USA], First Edition, February, 1996, pp: 132-154.

on 'urban traditional sector', 'Informal Sector' and 'Petty Commodity Production Sector'. In a broad sense, the contributions, which enlarge this literature, are of two categories:

In the first category, petty traders, casual labours, manufacturers of tiny sector, journeymen and the like have been considered as 'marginal section' of the labour force with particular attention either to the process of or to the forces responsible for such marginalisation.

While in the other category, the characteristic of the capitalist sector has been outlined as a harmony of interest with its continuum. Hence, any deviation from this basic harmony can be tinkered by implementing 'minor socio-economic policies'.

The latter category is fairly open for criticism whilst the former offers much room for in depth study. One such study might be centred round the question,

" HOW DOES THE MARGINALISED MASSES ORGANISED THEMSELVES AT WORK?" This issue demands exploration from two specific aspects:

From a practical point of view, it is essential to know the productivity, organisation, level of skill and entrepreneurial ability before going to implement any policy for assisting the low-income urban populace. Since, very often, they are negatively appraised from this point of view. While at the political level, it is of utmost importance to review the possibility of material upliftment that these people may or may not achieve and to overhaul the role that they themselves play or could play in the prevailing environment. This paper attempts to highlight the organisation of the garbage pickers who work daily at Bantala, one of the major dumping grounds in city of Calcutta, India.

Barring a few exceptions, there is a good resemblance between a typical industrial work place and Bantala garbage dump. Any visitor may sketch the following picture: About six hundred rag-tag and bobtail are at work as busy as bees. Countless vultures, dogs and specially flies surround them. The latter is so numerous that it is impossible to talk without a constant flapping of hands. The garbage pickers are commonly known as the KANGALIS—an allusion of living in the marginal pole. Well, at the first glance, this image might not be symmetrical to that of a secured industrial worker. Still, they can be so described as neither the scavengers nor their work is so isolated and sundered from the industrial sector as we might believe.

In fact there are a "...very close ties that link the garbage pickers to the big industry" [(a)]. Frankly, the garbage pickers are not the personnel of the CMC, [The Calcutta Municipal Corporation] nor they are directly connected with garbage collection. The responsibility of the latter rests with the Directorate of Conservancy, the CMC, which has a fleet of 118 trucks and its own labour force – collecting garbage according to its own schedule [(b)] and disposing of the same in the municipal dumping grounds. The garbage pickers are the most essential part of a recycling network, which feeds some large-scale factories in and around Calcutta's industrial belt. Materials like iron, paper, tin, plastic, glass, rag, leather, scrap metal, rubber etc. are collected in bulk quantity from the garbage dump and supplied to the industrial sector through numerous middlemen. So far as Calcutta's case is considered the garbage pickers are the major suppliers of recuperated material. The nature of this linkage between the garbage pickers and the industrial consumer of recuperated material can be summed up, as the former are the primary job executors of the latter without any employee – employer relationship. The former enjoys privilege in work – when to work, how to work, how long to work and when not to – an image of 'self-employed'. But this image is caged as the most vital factor, i.e., the industrial consumers control the prices of recuperated materials. From practical point of view, these 'self-employers' sell their labour power, an essentially contradictory nature of their class location [(c)].

The garbage dumps are, therefore, the place where the initial work starts and ends finally in the large-scale production sector. At this initial point, there is the absence of job contracts, supervisors or overseers, yet the work garbage picking' is regulated and organised in an informal way. The garbage is collected, sorted, bundled and sold with a certain degree of 'management' on the part of the initial buyers of the recuperated material. The prevailing conditions of work make the pickers bound to develop competitive attitude through some informal mechanism. They could be defined as the working concourse operating in such a manner as to satisfy the needs of the large industrial 'bosses' [for an approximation, please see the last column of **TABLE [1:19]**.

This paper starts with the delineation of recuperative work, specifically, it's past and the reasons behind it's transformation to present state. It is followed by a short notes on the activity of collecting and dumping of work as found in teh Bantala dumping ground. Our attention is devoted to garbage, as performed by the CMC from time to time and on the major dumping grounds of Calcutta. Next, we take up an overall discussion about organisation of the nature of organisation of such work, specifically, how far it is 'formal' and the stages when it is beyond 'formal'. We then present the socio-economic features of the garbage pickers with an emphasis on the internal and the external barriers that compel them in this precarious existence. Finally, the organised efforts among the garbage pickers of Bantala have been narrated with acumen into the permanency of such 'efforts'.

Recuperative Work

The city of Calcutta has witnessed industrial development within and around its jurisdiction upto late '60's. Due to a number of reasons, deterioration starts from early '70's. The situation has not yet been revived. As a consequence, substantial portions of the growing labour force are left outside the scope of employment in the formal sector. At present, a large number of workers are sheltered in the unorganised sector and carrying out vivid activities including garbage picking.

Garbage picking is one of the 'traditional' means of survival. The recuperative work, itself, has been changed in types and nature during the last three decades. Accordingly, the pickers adjust themselves with this transition. At the beginning, the work was mostly performed by the evacuees who moved along the streets and occasionally on the dumping ground in search of domestically generated garbage like spoon, cutlery, shoes, pot etc. which were destined for the low-income households through minor processing. After some period, a market for certain recuperated materials began to emerge. These are glass, tins & iron. For example, the former, through processing was sold to the laboratories and cosmetic manufacturing factories. Finally, the development of large-scale industries with their growing scarcity of raw materials brought forth a significant change in the aspect of recuperation. Mere collection of some particular items had been converted to purposeful and voluminous collection of additional new items like plastics, rags, papers, scrap metals etc. this is the posterior to the shift in demand from household to industrial sector. This aspect is predominating till now which make the growth of a number of recycling companies inevitable. These companies are concerned mainly with industrially generated garbage and rarely with domestic waste.

It is difficult to implement capital-intensive technology for recuperating materials directly from garbage due to its nature. Besides, it requires a large amount of capital so as to make such an implementation possible. This is the reason why both the CMC and the recycling companies have not yet been involved directly. Most of the municipal dumping grounds of Calcutta remain as a 'free land' only for the garbage pickers. However, if in the near or far future, sophisticated technologies were to come, there would be no more garbage pickers. More clearly, the presence of garbage pickers is due to the non-application of modernisation. The fact, therefore, comes to light is that the degree of accessibility of garbage is a depending factor and the future of the garbage picker is quite bleak, as the CMC is considering a number of proposals for utilizing the garbage for some specific purposes.

It is notable that besides dumping grounds, there are numerous garbage pickers working in different streets of Calcutta. Our calculation suggests that only in north and central Calcutta there are about 500 garbage pickers who work at the local vats and collection points. This type of garbage pickers are concerned with domestic garbage. They collect materials when garbage bring from household through handbarrows for disposing of either at the vats or at the collection points. They are very much conscious about the time when the municipal truck arrives for collecting garbage and hence collect the materials before such arrival. One of the peculiar facts is there is a clear cut delimitation based on area amongst the garbage pickers of this type and one never intrudes into others area.

In true sense, these garbage pickers are the most vulnerable section. "If anyone is to have their work interrupted or severely hindered, it is these people" [(d)]. They exist precariously but represent a workshop, which is more arranged than first impressions would warrant.

The Dumping Activity and the Major Dumping Grounds of Calcutta

Since early '20's, the CMC has been officially carrying out the work of collecting and dumping of garbage. From then on, the city of Calcutta has been subjected to different systems, namely, bull cart system, container system, dumper system and compactor system. At the very beginning, there was meter guage line from Maulali starting point to Dhapa dumping ground; when bull cart, stopping at the platform, disposed of garbage manually in the small wagon, which in turn, disposed of the same manually at Dhapa dumping ground. This system was continued up to 1952. After that, tripping truck has been introduced for unloading garbage through Tiffin gear [one kind of hydraulic equipment] though loading of garbage in the tripping truck was done manually. In '78, the pay loader has been introduced for loading of garbage mechanically in the tipping truck. Till now, both the former and the latter are in operation, which according to official sources save considerable time for loading and unloading of garbage. It seems that mechanical process is inevitable for a busy and congested city like Calcutta.

At present, Bantala is the largest [e] as well as the busiest dumping ground of Calcutta. It is situated on the eastern side, beside the eastern metropolitan bypass and adjacent to Salt Lake, Tangra and Ballygunge and at about 6 Km from Esplanade,-the heart of the city. The CMC started its operation in Bantala in '64 – '65. Besides, the CMC had two more major dumping grounds, namely, Kadapara and Dhapa. The former one had been closed in the early '72 after a continuous dumping of seventeen years.[f] It was used for dumping garbage of north and east Calcutta. In '76, this dumping ground was handed over to the Calcutta Improvement Trust, which turned it into public garden so as to beautify the gateway of Salt Lake.

Dhapa, another major dumping ground of the CMC, had been closed in 1979, though it is still being used only on emergency such as when for technical reason, the bulldozer at Bantala is not in a condition to level the garbage etc. According to the official source, Dhapa had been used regularly for a period of not less than sixty years. However, a countable portion of this dumping ground had already been occupied by the local peasants who started up the cultivation of vegetables like cauliflower, brinjal, radish, cabbage, onion etc. and commercial gardening of flowers specially merry gold, dahlia, heliotrope and a variety of seasonal flowers (such vegetables and flowers are highly attractive due to their size and freshness) without paying any land charges to the CMC. Initially the latter did not opposed because such activities i) would make the environment free from pollution and ii) would enhance the food production. But, now the CMC is thinking seriously for imposing land charges on these illegal cultivator.

Bantala was previously a very low quagmire. The CMC started its dumping operation at this place with a view to raise the level of the land. At present, the garbage of about whole Calcutta other then the following six wards, namely, Jadavpur, Behala, Garden Reach, Shyambazar, Bagbazar and Cossipore(g) are being dumped in Bantala. The process being operated at Bantala is known as land filling. It involves the disposal of garbage from municipal trucks and when it attains a certain height, using bulldozers flattens it. The attitude of the authorities to the garbage pickers is indifferent. Neither do they apply any force for driving out the latter nor do they undertake any responsibility for accident, which may easily take place at the time of collection of materials from garbage. In other words, both the workers and their work is impartially viewed by the authority.

And it is within this that the garbage pickers go on working.

The Work

As there exists a fixed hours of working in any workshop, likewise in the garbage dump, the pickers maintain a time schedule. They start work after 7 a.m when the garbage trucks begin to appear. The peak time is in between 9 a.m to 1 p.m when both the frequency of trucks as well as the number of pickers increase. This is the time when the recuperative work is carried on in full swing. Besides, the first fortnight of September and the first week of November is considered as a good season [h], when the percentage of garbage pickers raise by 25% to 30%. The CMC, however, dumps garbage every day in three shifts[i] other than those days when general strike is called by any political party.

The pickers including members of the same family work independently. There is no division of labour amongst the pickers. The work of picking garbage has the following steps: collection, sorting, putting in a heap and bundling up. Each picker carries out these activities separately in different parts of the day. It is amazing why the total work is so organised. After having a discussion, it appears that each picker respects his fellow individually but does not rely on teamwork or on partnership. The necessary equipages of this work are: a small, thin iron stick and a sack or basket. With these, the pickers collect materials when municipal trucks dispose garbage and even after the bulldozer flattens it. They collect everything, which could have some value: plastic, iron, tin, glass, leather, paper, rag, scrap metal etc. The collected materials are put inside the sacks or baskets temporarily and whenever the latter get filled up, these are emptied in a separate place known as GADI. Each picker has own GADI within the dump where sorting is done later in the day. Generally collection goes on up to 2 p.m to 2.30 p.m and sorting starts thereafter. The materials like rags, tins, rubber etc are put in a heap and bundled off while paper and plastic are packed neatly. At about 3.30 p.m to 4 p.m, selling of materials starts. Buyers of rags and leather have their own shelter within the dumping ground. The other types of materials are generally brought in Tangra, which is adjacent to Bantala through handcart where a number of shops for buying

TABLE 1.19

A Titbit About the Recuperative Work

Name of the material	*Price per Kg. [in Rs.]*	*Daily collection [in tonne: approx]*	*Recycling CO's Situated at*	*Final consumer*
Paper	.60	2.5	Shobhabazar & Bhangar	Paper industries for manufacturing pasteboard, tissues etc.
Iron	3.70	0.7	Baguihati, Murari Pukur and Beliaghata	Iron Workshop for manufacturing sheet iron, haft, etc.
Glass	.55	0.4	Dakshin Dari and Dum Dum Park	Cosmetic factories and laboratories as container
Plastic [Soft]	18.50	1.2	Bara Bazar	Toy making and utensil industries for manufacturing dolls and variety of utensils.

Table 1.19 contd...

Name of the material	*Price per Kg. [in Rs.]*	*Daily collection [in tonne: approx]*	*Recycling CO's Situated at*	*Final consumer*
Tin	1.30	1.8	Metiabruz and Cossipur	Foundries for metal casting and industries which manufacture corrugated iron, box, etc
Rag	.40	3.0	Ultadanga	Large scale industries for shaking off dust from machines and by the petty labourers for leaning the dirty spot off their bodies caused by lubricating oil.
Leather	.85	1.6	Tiljala & Tapsia	Leather industries for manufacturing slipper bags etc.

recuperated materials are situated. There is no written contract between the pickers and the buyers. The pickers are, therefore, at liberty to sell to the buyer who offers maximum price. All of these materials are sold according to weight other than battery, which is sold on piece-rate. After 5 p.m the activity on dump starts to decrease and the unsold materials especially straw and wood are taken home to be used as fuel. By nightfall, every picker returns home.

The materials, which are sold to the buyers either at Tangra or on the spot at Bantala, ultimately find their way for industrial consumption either in or around Calcutta's industrial zone except in a particular case.[j] It is difficult to get any precise notion about the quantity of materials so collected and sold every day. However from field surveys the following information has been gathered: [k]

The above table (Table: 1.19) exhibits the necessities and productivity of recuperated materials. The point to be noted is the work 'recuperation' is based on poverty. To highlight the latter, the income of the garbage pickers may be considered. The average daily income is in between Rs. 7 to Rs. 9, with some earning as little as Rs. 2.50 to Rs. 4, and other as much as Rs. 13 to Rs. 14 [1]. Within these limits, the pickers earn their living in a most arduous condition.

The ultimate buyers i.e., the factories that buy it fix the price paid for the recuperated material. There is a notable difference between the price paid by the latter and the price received by the garbage pickers due to the existence of numerous middlemen who expropriate lion's share by simple dealing with the selling and purchasing of waste materials. Any amelioration of these poor earnings of the garbage pickers too depends on the competition between the buyers. For example, when buyers of one particular product increase the price but other's do not, the pickers earn a bit more by supplying that product to the particular buyer. As a result, other buyers will get a little of that product. Naturally, they will also attract the garbage pickers by raising the price level. In short, higher the degree of competition between the buyers, higher will be the benefit for the garbage pickers. But such competition takes place occasionally.

Within this framework, it can also be explained that the garbage pickers are little more than daily labours. Whenever, there are casual vacancies in a number of workshops, the latter will be working for one who offer highest wages i.e., would have to leave the offers of others. But, so far as the case of garbage pickers is considered, they always collect a variety of materials. Whenever there would be an increment of price by any factory for a particular material, the pickers will be encouraged to collect that certain material, besides collecting other materials, i.e., they may work, both for the highest and the lowest paid factories at the same time.

However, the existence of a number of buyers also hides the presumable exploitative relationship between the pickers and the buyers. Such relationship could have been mirrored clearly if there were a monopoly buyer (as in case of mango-stones). Nevertheless, in course of survey, we have come across the following information: the prices of paper as received by the pickers represent only 20% than what is actually paid by the final consumers and that of rag and glass short by about one-seventh and one-fifth respectively.

As this price difference is well known to the pickers, the latter also, in turn, counter this realised fact in such ways as may be regarded 'unfair'. For instance, leather, rag and paper are made weighty either by sprinkling water or by keeping brickbat inside the sack. Whatever might be the reason, the 'selling' period is always marked by heated discussion between buyers and pickers with the former gain always by robbing the latter from 'true weight' irrespective of the latters' 'unfair means'. The latter is the looser in terms of weight and as such in terms of earnings also. Still the picker sells and will remain be a seller as they cannot go without earnings whatever little it might be. And this is the point to be emphasized. Since birth these people are enured with nothing but perennial poverty. It is the marginal stage of poverty, which upgrades their efficiency, productivity and the power of survival.

The 'primary' level of recuperative work, as evidenced in the Bantala dumping ground, can be described as a 'semi-formal' organisation of work [(m)]. The initial steps like collection, sorting and packing of materials from garbage have a good resemblance with the operation of likewise ordinary jobs in any industrial establishment. There, too, is the existence of simple manual operation and routined allocation of time – tenure in such a way as we find amongst the garbage pickers of Bantala. So, up to this portion, the nature of organisation of work is formal.

But, it would be somewhat debatable to call the organisation of the other steps of recuperative work i.e. buying and selling of waste materials as 'formal'. The non-existence of any agreement, placement of orders etc. on the part of buyers and sellers may not conform to the common buying and selling procedure of any industrial establishment. Hence, organisation of this portion of the work is beyond 'formal'.

TABLE 1.20

Socio-Economic Features of the Garbage Pickers of Bantala Dumping Ground, Calcutta

Criteria	*% Approx*	*Criteria*	*% Approx*
Sex: Male	71	**Experience:**	
Female	29	1-3 yrs.	32
		4-9 yrs.	11
		10-15 yrs.	49
		16-20 yrs.	5
		Above 20 yrs.	3
Religion:			
Hindu	62		
Muslim	31		
Unknown	7		
Age:		**Status:**	
5-12 yrs.	28	Married	59
13-19 yrs.	17	Unmarried	37
20-35 yrs.	43	Cohabit	4
36-50 yrs.	7		
Above 50 yrs.	5		
Permanent Residence:		**Education:**	
In Calcutta	16	Nil 57	
Outside Calcutta	73	1-2 yr. Primary	35
Outside West Bengal	11	2-3 yr. Primary	8
		Above primary	0

The Garbage Pickers

Frankly, the work of collecting materials from garbage is open to anybody. In order to have an insight about the garbage pickers, it seems worthwhile to realise the basic socio-economic features of this community. In our survey, we have interviewed 67 garbage pickers working presently at the Bantala dumping ground. The following table illustrates the results thereof.

The above table draws out certain attractive features, which should be considered with the reason behind. First, religion is unknown to about seven percent pickers. In particular, pickers of this category are orphans. These 'religion free' people are also 'education free'. How could we define these 'beneath the stair' living people? A human being without any so-called 'formal' symbol of religion and education? Again, among the Hindu – the Kaora, Dom, Palukato and Muchis – i.e. the lower as well as the untouchable castes are predominant. Second, there is an exodus specially in the 'teen' ages in search of higher urban income which includes a variety of occupations ranging from cycle van driving, porterage, daily labour, peddling to even cadgeing in the shopping centres of Calcutta. However, according to the old garbage pickers, these 'adventures' of early age are equally balanced by retrocession in the latter period due to the comparative precarious earnings in those occupations than garbage picking [n].

Third, there is the presence of a substantial number of 'migrant' pickers of rural Bengal. [About three-forth of the total number of pickers]. The pickers of this category take a temporary shelter near the Bantala dumping ground who are, in fact, the JOGALIS (a helper for all types of rural work like farming, animal – husbandry, gardening etc.) and in the good season a countable portion of this category go back to their native villages to act as a JOGALI. They utilise this source of earnings only when there is depression in other sources of casual earnings. Fourth, the pickers of middle age and of above fifty are countable in numbers. In the above table, there is altogether twelve percent pickers only who are within this age bar. This is understandable. The work of picking materials from garbage primarily requires the ability to endure strong sun, heavy rain or biting cold as well as the even present stench of garbage and the hurry to reach the garbage before others when it is dumped from municipal trucks. Besides, the quick collection of waste materials may also be added. In their early age, the pickers contribute an inhuman labour which, in turn, makes them unfit in their later life. Their sons or daughters somehow support the 'lucky' pickers while the luckless continue for life. Fifth, the level of education is, as expected, very negligible. It needs no explanation but a simple comment. All their efforts are spent in earning the means of living and nothing is left for any other activity, be it education or leisure. Finally, in course of the survey, we noticed a very few pickers who had been in casual employment in the sewerage department of the CMC. These pickers are seriously expecting a call back by the CMC to work permanently. If it comes true, they would be in a better off condition. But, in their own version, it may take any time between one year to one decade. Nevertheless, they can be differentiated from other pickers in a sense that might they have a chance for betterment in future.

But what about the majority of pickers? It would be improper to think that they are always setting their hearts up to any job elsewhere, rather, it is the fact that the majority of pickers like to utilise all possible chances within this activity [other than the 'adventurous' teenagers]. They like to work 'for themselves' where they have no obligation to any third party.

The pickers around twenty/twenty five years of age are the most satisfied persons in the dump. They earn more due to their physical capacity to fulfil the 'primary requirement' of this work mentioned already. They are the 'hopes' of the youngish pickers while the oldster, not being able to compete with the young, are generally found in such 'spot' where dumping has already been closed. As such bulldozers had leveled 'spot' for some years ago, they are to dig it for searching whether there is waste material. Mostly they are disheartened but time and again they carry on digging till sunset. Is it simply a keen desire for survival or from up side down, an innovative effort at the same time?

One part of the Bantala dumping ground has taken the shape of a hillock by the dumping of the remains of once ignited coal used as fuel by numerous industries of Calcutta. Here, we find a notable concentration of female pickers who collect the coal dust. The city of Calcutta is experiencing a constant increase in the price of coal, which is, in turn, a headache for the low-income household so far as the consumption of fuel is considered. However, at present, this problem is well tackled by the use of GUL (a cheap substitute of coke-briquette) which is manufactured mainly by the use of coal dust supplied by these pickers. In fact, the pickers of waste materials can be emmarked as 'entrepreneur' in a sense that they are exploiting the least possibilities of a variety of uncommon items.

The experience one could have from this 'informal workshop' goes in favour of individual dynamism. But this quality so far as their regular earnings are considered, does not pay a high dividend due to the existence of the following reason:

The quantity of material, which can be collected from garbage, is not unlimited. So it is doubtful whether the pickers would be in a better-off condition, if they contribute more labour. In spite of that, if they work hard, the total earnings may be increased by some negligible amount. Their working hours are related with the arrival of garbage trucks and once garbage is dumped, there is a fierce competition among them for acquiring the best material. It is the CHANGRAS (the nick name of the young pickers) who gain from such scramble. Naturally, the remaining pickers are left with materials of poor quality and low price. It can be remarked that, under the prevailing situation, more work may not always matched with more pelf.

In an exceptional case, however, a 'lucky' garbage picker earns 'windfall income'. It occurs particularly when materials are dumped directly from industries, universities or from the demolition of unauthorized hotels, restaurant etc. We have been informed by a picker how he had once occupied a heavy lot of costly scrap furniture's as an occurrence of the latter. Still, in their own version, "This might happen once in, say, four to five years". Hence, this type of purely 'pera adventure opportunities' should be excluded from regular earnings.

Due to the reason mentioned above the 'dynamic' garbage pickers are to be any thing but poor. The only break through is to become a buyer who earns comparatively a good margin through dealing with the waste materials. According to our survey, it requires an investment of something like nine hundred to one thousand rupees in order to be a 'standard' buyer who earns an average of rupees two hundred seventy five to rupees three hundred per week while a 'petty' buyer needs to invest an amount like rupees three hundred fifty to four hundred for an weekly average income of rupees ninety to one hundred. The former group, depending on reputation, obtains credit for financing their trade from the MAHAJAN (i.e. the wholeseller of this trade), which may extend to thirty percent. The 'petty' buyers, all of whom were once the garbage pickers, have arranged for working capital through savings from their past occupation.

Is it only the paucity of capital, which retards a picker to be a buyer? Or, practically to be a petty buyer? Well, our field experience does not agree with this. It is rather the case that this occupation is well characterised by a simultaneous promotion and demotion to buyer and picker respectively. Therefore, the proper question should be why couldn't the petty buyer able to maintain their buyership? This question is viable as it points out some of the constraints, which are inherent in this job and hence require an illustration in this regard. The first constraint is within the outlook of the garbage pickers. They do follow a peculiar convention in their family life even today—'the more the number of children' – with traditional belief – 'the more the number of earners' [o]. When, in fact, it is the excessive family burden that dries up the low margin of profit they earn as a 'petty' buyer of waste materials. The other constraints are the outside factors of which the important are: The police authority always suspects their JHUPRIS (literally shack) as a centre of 'smuggled' and 'contraband' goods and make frequent search for the same when the obvious way-out is either to pay bribe or to be tortured by them. Besides, the degrees of 'adjustment' with the 'standard' buyers determine the time tenure of 'petty' buyership.

For a better look through, let us relate the case of a garbage picker, which might as well be considered a common tale for the rest.

Some seventeen to eighteen years ago, Samsur Ali came to Bantala and started his life as a garbage picker. He has seven brothers and sisters along with his father and mother. They were somehow sheltered in a JHUPRI in Tangra made by bamboo-cane and thatched by waste pollythene and plywood of poor quality. Most of his family members joined with him while one of his brothers went to Dakhin Dari in the northeast Calcutta and adopted a different way of living. For the first five years, he had been I) introduced with different facet of this occupation, particularly, regarding its buying operation ii) a victim of unnecessary police marking for several times and iii) in a condition to merely survive without any savings. Some ten years ago, he became a 'petty' buyer for the first time. This was possible through hard won savings for two years. He had a favourable time then when he could remember that the ALLAH (The Almighty GOD) was so kind to him so as to gift him once a silver candelabrum in the dumping ground. He got married at that time. It lasted for nearly two years. The deterioration started from an incident when Sarmsur had been badly involved in a tussle with an influential 'standard' buyer in Tangra who tried to rob him while weighing the materials. He took a decision of closing his relation with than influential `standard' buyer. Sometimes around the same period, he had been informed that some of the 'standard' buyers of Tapsia offered better price for waste materials than that of Tangra. He then used to supply there but as Tapsia is comparatively at a far distance that Tangra, he had to bear a considerable amount of carrying cost. Soon after, he realised that his total earnings came down sufficiently than before. Again, he tried to make a normal relation with the 'standard' buyers of Tangra who then, as they were aware of Samsur's 'new relation' at Tapsia, took a revenge by offering him a price even lower than the price they were paying to other petty buyers right then. "It was due to the former mistake I committed and is a common mistake being committed by other petty buyers always'. This utterance of Samsur actually points out the poor subordinative relation between the 'standard' and the 'petty' buyers of Tangra. In order to have an overall control on Bantala dumping ground, the former is always alert. One of the standard buyers of Tangra openly remarks, "You see, if we are to keep our interest, any potential relation between these petty buyers and the buyers other than ourselves must be stopped. Otherwise, in near future, it will be as fatal as to wind up our own business. Of course, within Tangra, they could sell anyone". It, therefore, graphs their mentality in toto: The petty buyers would have to confine in Tangra as well as to adjust with the usual malpractice of the 'standard' buyers regarding weights and prices. In true sense, they are in an impasse. The position of Samsur become worse when his mother during that crucial period was declared a patient of tuberculosis. Samsur finished the little amount of capital that he accumulated so far through medical treatment. Finally, he had no other way then to revert back to garbage picking. During the last eight years, he had been upgraded to 'petty' buyer twice and failed to maintain it. At the time of this interview, though he has again became a 'petty' buyer, is likely to become a picker very soon. As his father is now suffering from a bad injury in the waist caused by a police torture some two months ago, Samsur is bearing an average of thirty rupees as medical expenses every fortnight. He has four children and his bibi (wife) is still carrying one. One of his brothers, owing to an accident, has lost both of his legs and becomes a permanent burden. In addition, police marking has not been ceased though it has been minimized to some extent and Samsur is yet to make an adjustment with the 'standard' buyers of Tangra.

The case of Samsur clearly enumerates that the stagnation of the pickers and the petty buyers of Bantala dumping ground perpetually strengthens the 'standard' buyers of Tangra. It is also a bit of a wonder that they consider such an exploitative relation is as natural as the earth moves round the sun. They point out Satya Lod, Thakur Paramanick and a few others who became rich men from this occupation fairly long ago. Such 'successful' pickers who are now in a different trades and having own land, house etc., are still remembered by these pickers. The petty buyers irrespective of their hopeless position urge the aspirations of the garbage pickers by proving that there is a little more money to earn that the latter usually earn. It is not surprising, therefore, that the former is viewed as the prevailing milestone by the latter. The impact of such apparently successful legend is so predominant so as to keep any revolution amongst the garbage pickers of Bantala a mile's apart.

However, it would be improper to suggest that the garbage pickers being a part of the economic system do not attack it mainly due to their estimation about the possibility of improvement falls short of reality. Such an advice would be nothing but an oversimplification. Of course, there are many garbage pickers who are satisfied with their present work. They think little about progress and care a fig about future. One would be in a trouble to sketch the mentality of the garbage pickers. On the one hand, there is a picker like Suku. He has three children and he likes to get them educated. He has a little bit of savings and, in his opinion, if the could maintain the same rate of savings, he would be the owner of a cycle can within two years and will let it on hire. He has some constructive ideas, which he likes to fulfil. Reverse is the case of Joydev. During the last fifteen years, he had been oscillated between picker and petty buyer for a number of times. He is highly addicted to gambling and smoking GANJA AND BHANG (types of dry leaves consumed for inebriation). He is of peculiar nature. If he earns some money in the afternoon, he takes some loan from some of his fellows at the same time and spends all in gambling, and if he wins, loses all in drinking or in smoking. But, he never refuses to help any of his fellows be it monetary or otherwise when they are in distress. He is even to go on starvation as a consequence of repayment of loan. Sometimes, he is so daring to leave work for some days and remains shiftless.

Joydev is not an exception. There are other pickers also who go to work for the first two days and either loiter or remain intoxicated for the next two days. How could we interpret this attitude? Are they too wise to know the hardship required for fulfilling any mission, be it money or anything else? Hence, without hankering after any impossibility, they live in penury, remain indifferent in penury and do not mourn for being living in penury'.

Does it, at the same time, an impartial outlook to their life also?

The Organised Efforts

It is due to the inherent features and the ideology of work that evolve within the dumping complex, which make the pickers to interact in different ways either with other pickers or with the outsiders. As we know little about the organisation of work among the marginalized masses, our first impression might warrant them as the workers who are in a constant conflict and keen competition with each other and so incapable of being organised. To some extent, this view is intrinsic specially when there prevails piecework system, which actually motivates one worker to fight against another worker. Highlighting this particular aspect, Karl Marx wrote, "... the wider scope that piece wages give to individuality tends to develop the competition of the workers with each other."[p] The dumping ground is a spectacular example of the independent capacity of the garbage pickers where at times working conditions get hectic and rusty for grabbing the more valuable materials. It cannot be denied, however, there is the existence of both conflict and competition.

Nevertheless, to consider the garbage dump as a field open for violence and conflict is paradoxical. In the light of the environment prevalent in the dumping ground, conflict or violence rarely takes place, suggesting the solidarity of the garbage pickers, which one could witness in such place. The prima facie evidence is the total absence of snatching or robbing and even pilferage of waste materials in the dumping ground. The pickers pileup the waste materials in their own GADI without keeping a close eye on it. This is noticeable particularly if we consider how they could recognize their own GADI amidst the numerous similar GADI or detect the stolen materials when it is least possible. At times, the dumping ground witnesses impressive attitude of conciliation or arbitration amongst the garbage pickers on some problematic issues. In one occasion when two garbage pickers, Megha and Gopal, were in a tussle over the possession of a scrap mudguard, other pickers take up the matter seriously and settle it through dividing the possible earning the scrap mudguard could derive. So, collective action as and when needed, is not uncommon. In fact, there is on unwritten law among the pickers of the Bantala dumping ground. In case of any dispute, the contending pickers would have to abide by the judgment of other pickers working nearby. Besides, the garbage is not 'closed' for the new pickers. The freshers need not take extra trouble for occupying his place in the dumping ground or for selling materials directly to the buyers. The existing pickers care a little about whether or not their competitors are growing in numbers. In an indifferent mood, one of them remarked openly: "Why should we drive out a new comer who is also in distress like us?" It mirrors that kind of fellow feeling, which is dwindling in our material world.

In the winter of '82, a union among the garbage pickers of Bantala dumping ground was in the process of formation against the repressive action of the police authority, which was raised to an intolerable height then. Accordingly, about seventy garbage pickers with Babul as president and Hakil as secretary made a deputation to the local santi (literally peace) committee. The latter with sympathy considered the matter. Ultimately, a round table discussion was held between the latter and the police authority of Tangra police station sometimes in January '83. As a consequence, the police raid became surprisingly rare.

But, the good time did not last long. In course of time, police action again started though at a diminished rate of which Samsur's father is an example.

What conclusions could we reach after looking over all these incidents? The garbage pickers can act and react whenever circumstances, be it external or internal, demand so.

The above facts make it clear that the garbage pickers are able to organise themselves. So far as our field experience is considered, it is the petty buyers and obviously the standard buyers who possess maximum potential for organisation as they have comparatively some extra time and better earnings for executing the needful works. It is questionable whether these groups will be motivated in this context. The answer lies in the related interest that these people have in the garbage dump. Likewise the garbage pickers, the latter is also the basic source of earning for the former.

Nevertheless, it is doubtful whether any fundamental change will take place in the primary level of the recuperative work. First, the attitude of the garbage pickers make it perspicuous that other than the occasional cases, they are mainly interested to preserve their right to work and not to the prevailing conditions of work. Second, as a consequence of their peculiar mentality, many garbage pickers do not like to consider themselves as exploited. Atleast to a majority, petty buyership is highly desired and reckoned as a level of success when, in fact, it is an impasse and a most precarious level.

To sum up, there exists some sort of ephemeral unionism among the garbage pickers of Bantala so as to achieve some basic objectives. These could be marked as a counterveiling effect of the alarming situation as and when arises. But, in the absence of the latter, no such activity prevails. Therefore, it is still in question whether Bantala dumping ground will experience a permanent organisation of the garbage pickers concerned not only with the protection of right to access to the garbage but also with the betterment of earnings and working conditions.

Conclusion

Thus, we complete the description of a work complex, which by its nature of organisation of work is semi-formal. The garbage pickers are a bit more than the industrial daily labours. A true and fair picture about the solidarity of the garbage pickers emerges the existence of organisation, though need-based and transient. The whole gamut of the recuperative work as found in the Bantala dumping ground is self-depending. The organisation of work is characterised by two extreme elements: In one side, there is tranquility in general and respect to each other while on the other side there is occasional conflict and mistrust towards each other to act as a group.

The entire community of the garbage pickers is poverty-striken, though at the micro-level there is a clear indication of entrepreneurial ability and innovative capacity. The attitudes of the garbage pickers are either to go ahead by making money, as a section of them are motivated to preserve in the hope of becoming buyers or to pass somehow. It is due to the effect of the latter that the pickers are concerned mainly to defend their right to work.

The garbage pickers, as realised in course of the survey, are productive, skilled, enterprising and also to some extent organised. But the way the prevailing structural constraints interact is sufficient to blot out the potentials that might improve the livelihood of the garbage pickers. The latter, through their activities in the dumping ground, support their means of survival, but, at the same time, play a dominant role for the industrial economy by providing a supply of necessary inputs. Stressing particularly on this point, we could solicit for ameliorative programmes, which will bring stability in the primary level of the recuperative work and enhance the level of income of those workers.

In this regard, one could refer to the proposals, which are at present under consideration by the CMC. There is a proposal from Burn Standard Company for setting up one biogas plant adjacent to the Bantala dumping ground. The implementation of this, is expected to take place in near future. The garbage pickers might find employment provided their experience and skill is considered 'worthy' for absorption by the respective authorities.

Take a look apart from it. The true position of the garbage pickers is in the lower echelons of capitalism. They render service wholly to the industrial consumer of waste materials while, in turn, the latter accepts no social responsibilities towards these workers. How to make the garbage pickers aware of this – they are not in a casual but in the primary and inseparable fringe where from industrial production starts – it is an issue that demands further exploration from the social scientists in future. But, at present, we might reasonably solicit for extensive study that will search for the potentials so as to utilise the productivity of these marginal labourers, be it within the confines of Bantala dumping ground or elsewhere.

REFERENCES

(a) C.H. Birkbeck: 'Vagrant Vultures or industrial worker'? Paper presented to the CLACSO employment – unemployment group seminar on 'The Urban Informal Sector' Santiago, Aug '77, found in 'The Urban Informal Sector' ed. by Ray Bromley: p: 1185.

(b) There are 57 vats in Calcutta where pay loader is in operation. Of these 14 and 13 vats are attended once in each odd date and in each even date respectively and the remaining 30 vats are attended at least twice daily.

Besides, there are 293 collection points in Calcutta; about 80% of these are collected at least once daily while the remaining are attended to every alternate day.

(c) For a full discussion of contradictory class location: See, E. Olin Wright 'class boundaries in advanced capitalist Societies' New Left Review, No: 78, July – Aug. '76, pp: 3-41.

(d) C. H. Birkbeck: *ibid.,* p. 1175.

(e) The Bantala dumping ground covers an area of 146.65 acres

(f) Information in this regard have been provided by Mr. A.K. Chakraborty, Chief Engineer, Department of Conservancy, The CMC.

(g) Out of these six wards, the garbage of Cossipore, Shyambazar and Bagbazar are dumped at Noapara dumping ground; It covers an area of 42.987 acres. Taratala and Tollygunj dumping grounds are used for dumping garbage of Jadavpur and Behala respectively while garbage of Garden Reach are dumped at Khidirpore dumping ground. All of these are minor dumping grounds and used for local dumping. There are altogether one hundred forty-one wards in Calcutta.

(h) Generally within the middle of September, Biswakarma Puja [festival] takes place. According to convention, every factory completes its annual cleaning before this occasion. While Diwali festival, which takes place generally within the first week of November, is the annual clean out period for the household sector by convention. As a consequence of these two occasions the quantity of garbage become bulky.

(i) The morning shift starts from 7 a.m. while the afternoon and evening shifts start from 12 noon and 5 p.m. respectively.

(j) One of the striking features of Bantala is the hue and cry amongst the pickers for collecting the stones of mangoes, which start from the late summer and continues up to the middle of the rainy season. So far as quantity is considered, about 70% of the total collection is then concentrated on this particular material. This is sold to a contractor who comes to Bantala only at that season. As we conduct this survey in a different period, we do not meet with this contractor. He is the only monopoly buyer of Bantala dumping ground who sends this material to South India for planting mango seedling.

(k) This survey was conducted during September-October, 1988

(l) One US dollar was valued at Rs. 15.42 as on 02.03.1989. SOURCE: THE STATESMAN. Now it is valued at Rs. 47.90 as on 12.04.2003. Source: ibid.

(m) Till date, the dichotomy formal/informal is based mainly on such criteria as exclusive guidance of law and order, registration of the unit, unionism among the workers etc. All of these are however debatable. First: there is tax evasion, adulteration, degradation of raw materials consumed in the production process etc., among those units, which are exclusively under the guidance of law and order. How could we define them? Formal or informal? Second, in India, there are numerous registered units, which are practically non-operating. There is no repeated buying and selling – the fundamental nature of business – in such units. Should we classify those units as 'formal' simply because they are 'registered'? Again, it requires at least seven workers to form a registered trade union according to the Indian Trade Union Act 1926. So there is no registered trade union of workers for those business units where the numbers of workers are less than seven. If unionism of workers is the criteria of `formal' sector, how could these units be categoried ?

We, therefore, find it morelogical to extract, as for as possible, the general manners involved in production and selling procedure as found in any industrial complex and to emphasize on these general manners instead of any rigid criteria as discussed above. In our opinion, an economic activity will be `formal' or `informal' according to its degree of conformity to these general manners.

For ref. (n), (o), (p), please see manuscript.

The author finds here an opportunity to express his graditude to Prof. Amitabha Gupta and Dr. Sanjukta Das for their esteemed services throughout this work.

Last but not the least, the hearty co-operaiton of Mr. Dharma Das Sarnakar and a number of garbage pickers will be mourned by the author forever.

5

Barriers to Development of the Informal Sector and Some Related Issues

> The growth of the informal sector suffers highly due to its complete subordination to the formal sector in both inputs and outputs markets. To outline the basic facts, the informal sector, due to the absence of bulk purchase and credit facilities, pays high price for the required inputs and receives low price for it's product whether wage goods, subcontract or personal services, as the output market is dominated by the formal sector. Besides, there is fierce competition among the producers of the informal sector and a prejudice to prefer formal sector products. All of these are the obstacles for the growth of the informal sector, which must be considered while prescribing any ameliorative policies for this sector.

Preamble

The informal sector units are facing a lot of troubles for imperfection in different markets, namely, product, factor, labour and capital. A joint trade union movement in this sector is also a matter of guess work. Yet, this sector will survive in the structural opposition to the formal sector.

The Obstacles

Generally speaking, informal sector, as noticed in the developing countries, is in an impasse. It exists in the lower echelons of capitalism. The total process of accumulation is determined outside the informal sector of which it has no control. Likewise, the capacity of accumulation of capital in the informal sector is limited due to its limited access to modern inputs and to product markets. The implication of this can be realised easily. The lack of access to basic inputs of production (as the input markets are monopolized by the formal sector) determines that informal sector can operate only with the residual resources, which, in turn, keep this sector away from any possibility of technological upliftment.

Again, due to the limited access to product markets which are dominated by the oligopolistic firms of the formal sector, the possibilities of expansion for the informal sector is subordinated.

Product market subordination and limited access to basic inputs are reinforced by different mechanisms on the informal sector in such a way the surplus generated by the latter is extracted from it. These mechanism can be identified in the exorbitant price of the inputs (paid by the informal sector) and in the lower price of the outputs (received by the informal sector). The difference is reaped by the formal sector. (Bose '74, Bienefeld '75).

Therefore, due to this market constraint, the informal sector serves as a cheap labour outlet for the formal sector. The units operating within the formal sector obtain the surplus at the production level.

The degree of dependence and the direction of the links vary according to the types of goods. For example: the agricultural sector is the main supplier the raw foodstuffs. The latter comes to the market either directly through open market operation or through wholesales. But in case of textiles or processed foods, there is a direct link with the manufacturers or whole sellers of the formal sector.

On the output side, the subordination linkage operates through different channels. Firstly: the sale of wage goods, which, in turn, help to swell the degree of exploitation. Secondly: the subcontracting. In this case, the informal activities, which sell their output to large firms of the formal sectors generally, receive a smaller price than the labourers who carry out the same function within the formal sector. Thirdly: the sale of personal services which is characterised by a small and stagnant returns due to the scarcity of additional job opportunities and low income elasticity.

However, there is subordination in both input and output market. The price at which the informal sector purchases inputs is generally higher due to the small quantity purchased and the non-existence of credit facilities. On the other hand, the sale price of output is lower due to the fact that the entire output market is controlled by the formal sector.

Besides, there is the existence of a bias, which goes against the consumption of the informal sector's products. This is evidenced within the formal sector. As a consequence, the rate of growth of the informal sector suffers to a large extent.

It is evident from above that the lack of access to resources and product markets causes for a limited capacity of accumulation and thus of expansion of the informal sector.

There are clear and considerable links between formal and informal sector in the context of purchasing and selling of inputs and outputs respectively. This link can be viewed as one of domination and subordination. There is no equality either in the extent of or in the nature of this link.

In addition to above, severe competition [a] and accelerating differentiation among the informal sector's producers together with the proliferation of small workshops and micro trading concerns have an incremental effect on the problems confronting most of the working masses in obtaining adequate access to the means of subsistence. Due to these reasons, the informal units are forced to under utilise their available skills, to use inputs of low quality and to suffer from grave restriction on their capacity to even reproduce their present conditions.

Factors Responsible for the Survival of the Informal Sector

The informal sector, as evident in our above discussion, is confronted to a lot of obstacles. Consequently, one might consider that such impediments would have an impact to reduce the informal sector activities in the long run. But, as there is the continual existence of some particular factors in the developing country's economy, the informal sector will exist for good.

In this regard, on might refer to a study [b] which was centered round the question like "what will happen within the commercial sector, since competition between different productive units could lead to a decrease in informal commercial activities?" This was anticipated for the first time by Sansone ('77) [c] His study enlightens the factors for which the informal sector not only survives but also acquires the competency to vie with the modern units of the formal sector.

Though it is true that there is an overall increase in the market share of the formal sector, but nevertheless, a declining trend of the informal commercial activities is yet to be noticed (as it was anticipated by Sansone '77).

The price differentials between the modern units and the informal units should be considered in this respect. The study, [d] mentioned above, revealed the fact that such differentials vary according to the types of products [e] and are not homogeneous.

The price differentials can be analysed with the help of the following factors: Firstly, a certain part of the price differentials are normal deviation in commerce, Secondly, 'quality' plays a good role in such differentials and Thirdly, for evaluating price differentials 'location' and 'proximity' of the competing units should not be left outside.

Considering all these factors, it can be said that the informal small units will survive and will retain demand even in the face of competition due to the prevailing imperfections both in the product and the factor markets.[f] For a better understanding, it can be discussed separately as under:

Imperfections in the Product Market

Imperfection in the product market is the result of demand compartmentalisation due to various factors. These need some features of the productive units, which are most common to the informal small shops than the modern units of formal sector like super markets. The poor purchasing power of the masses along with their income fluctuation and the need to consume a basket of goods with some diversification induce a particular type of demand. One of the characteristics of such type of demand is regular purchasing of a variety of goods at a lower quantity.

This type of demand has a direct effect on the production unit. Because, as a consequence of this effect, the latter turns to be such a unit which is characterised by the ability to sell in small fraction, little product-mix diversification and accessibility both in terms of location and business hours.

The above factors have an adverse effect on the earnings of the modern units of the formal sector. Because, technological change, so far as commerce being is considered, is highly related to economy of scale and product diversification. In order to ensure the former, particularly in an area where lower income group resides, there must be a considerable distance between the units. Small informal units dominate in such areas of the poor consumers because they could sell in as small quantities as required.

The question may arise as to why do the modern units of the formal sector cannot sell at a small quantity? The reason lies in the technological confinement since the maximum part of the profit of such units is earned through bulk purchasing and packing mechanically in standard units. This method, however, minimises labour in connection with sale.

The product-mix diversification required by the low-income household is very much limited either in terms of number of products or in terms of branches and qualities. The small informal shops in general keep the main products of a single quality. But for the modern shops of the formal sector product differentiation is the only way to compensate for those commodities where margin of profit is comparatively low.

As the frequency for purchasing goods in the lower income areas is relatively high, it requires that shops established in such areas must be accessible because both time and transport costs can change consumer's decisions. The general tendency of the modern shops of the formal sector is to select a location where higher income group resides. It is just the reverse for the small informal shops, which are established mostly in the area of lower income group. Besides, the modern shops of the formal sector are generally located either in the main street or in the shopping centres while the small informal shops are located in any areas ranging from secondary streets to narrow lanes where there is no public transport facility. The requirement of accessibility includes flexible and long business hours. The modern shops of the formal sector cannot compete with the small informal shops in this regard because of their limited business hours. The latter, however, remains open for a long hours everyday including Sunday.

Finally, the personal relation, which develops between the consumers and the owners of the small informal shops, should also be counted in this regard.

Such relationship is responsible for the imperfection of product market as it has an influence over the functioning of the market in various ways starting form assisting the customers to purchase the right products, to the possibilities of sending children to shops, meeting the neighbours, glancing over the newspapers. The consequence of this relationship is that it lets an opportunity for the owner of the small informal shops to estimate the credit worthiness of the customer.

The former, on a personal basis, gives credit to the latter, which, in turn, reinforces the small purchasing capacity of the clientele.

Imperfection in the Factor Markets

The products, which are sold by the small shopkeepers of the informal sector at a comparatively high price than the modern units of the formal sector, ensure a profit margin for the former. The advantage of the former, irrespective of high price they charge to the customer, is that there is no question of paying sales tax and surcharges. But, for the latter, no such benefit is available.

On the other hand, the modern units like super markets of the formal sector have several other advantages. They possess bargaining capacity and get discount for bulk purchasing as well as obtain credit facilities at better terms. The transport cost is minimum as most of them have their own vehicles. Besides, such units purchase directly from the producers in most cases, which has double benefits: Firstly, by avoiding the middlemen, they are getting the necessary products at a cheap rate and Secondly, they obtain discounts for buying in large quantities.

The above facts indicate that the gross margin would be much higher for the modern units of the formal sector due to the effect of both savings and discounts connected with purchase than that of the small shops of the informal sector. The question then arises: "How does the latter survive in the long run?"

To answer for it, imperfections of the factor markets should be analysed which are mainly related to the form of organisation and the production process of the small shops of the small shops of the informal sector. Here, one would have to recall the basic features of the latter. The units belonging to this sector are mostly family owned, majority of labours are self-employed and the production functions are closely related to the consumption function. The implicit factor prices are determined in a separate way in such units, which do not conform, to those existing for the production factors used in the rest of the economy. Due to this reason, the implicit price for labour is much lower in the informal sector (as there is the employment of family labour) than that of the formal sector. Besides, although the implicit cost of capital relative to the price of labour is higher due to the scarcity of capital, but the low capital requirement of the informal sector's units along with the dual use of capital (i.e. both for production and consumption) ensures a lower implicit cost for this factor also.

Imperfections in Labour Market

The wages of the paid workers of the informal units and that imputed to the unpaid family men is in no case greater than what they could earn if they are provided with job opportunity in the formal sector. The same view can also be expressed for the owners of the informal units who could have better earnings in the formal sector than their present income. Collins and Garrod ('71) made an interesting study in this respect. They found that even when sex, age, education and working hours are homogeneous, there is still a difference between the earnings of the informal unit owners and that of the self-employed in the rest of the economy.

It is questionable as to why do the informal units owners deprive themselves from a larger share of income what they could earn form the modern units of the formal sector? Apart from the availability of limited occupational opportunities and the adverse personal characteristics, which stand against mobility, the organisation of production on a family basis assists to retain their present position creating a type of labour market segmentation. If they shut down their present operation, the family members will be deprived of job opportunities who generally are not available for whole time jobs, as is the case for wife and children of school age who allocate their time amongst the study, the household duties and the production activities.

Imperfection in Capital Market

In the informal sector's unit, returns on Capital employed are, in fact, a part of the total implicit return. In other words, the actual business capital is lower than what it usually appears.

However, if the rate of return on investment of the informal sector's units is compared with that of the formal sector's units, it can be seen that capital is used more efficiently in the former sector than in the latter sector. The study (g) we referred above disclosed that monthly return on capital for the informal commercial establishments is 2.3% when for the super market such return is only 1.9%.

However, the informal unit owners cannot invest all his capital as the latter is used for both purpose, namely production and consumption. If the availability of capital for outward investment is limited, such unit owners, for the purpose of compensating his return on capital, would have to find a job for himself. Otherwise, he will not be able to upgrade himself in his present level of earning. In such a situation, there will be a problem for finding a suitable job for the unit owners. In addition, it will also restrict the job opportunities for the remaining family members. In short, it will create the same labour market problem, which we have discussed already.

Trade Unions in the Informal Sector

An organised movement of the workers of the informal sector may revive their condition. Though, the worker of this sector is characterised by non-unionism, but there is at least one exception. There exist a number of unions amongst the street traders of Calcutta. Let us illustrate how far they have been able to improve their working conditions through organised movement.

A considerable number of the street hawkers of Calcutta take their membership in any of the three registered trade unions[g1] presently established in this city. Of course, a portion of the members have valid trade licenses and permits. These trade unions are, in turn, affiliated to major political parties. Considerable doubts can be expressed regarding the roles such unions play amongst the 'independent' workers. The latter is neither the wage earners, nor they do have any well-defined employment relationship. Besides, most of the major trade union movements are not at all interested or linked to the hawker's unions. The trade unions of the street hawkers of Calcutta are yet to receive any major success in general. Although, such unions fix up a very low subscription for its members, nevertheless the latter is notably reticent to pay their dues. These unions are characterised by individualism, inefficiency and corruption particularly for the leadership. At least two other incipient trade unions of the hawkers of this city had been abolished during the last decade due to overall apathy, poor leadership, corruption and inefficiency. Every unions try to create pressure on the authorities to support only it's own members and there is conflict amongst these trade unions due to their affiliation to different political parties and, hence, receive patronage from different urban elite groups.

According to one spokesman of one of the hawkers unions, the metropolitan authority of Calcutta should not indulge those hawkers who are operating without any valid licenses and the membership of such illegal hawkers should be cancelled from the respective unions. It indicates that at least one union invites oppressive measures for being taken against the majority of hawkers; since, a majority of the hawkers are carrying out their jobs without any valid licenses.

Amongst these trade unions, there are some prosperous hawkers who have capital and experience and want to proceed towards a prestigious 'middle class' business. There is the total absence of 'sub proletarian solidarity', which is rather replaced by factionalism and self-interest in these unions. The activities of these unions are mainly centred for retaining or defending their rights to work rather than ameliorate the conditions and earnings of the work.

Another striking feature is that there is a little solidarity between the street hawkers and other sections of the urban poor. The hawkers unions of Calcutta represent a small and comparatively impecunious category than other trade unions of Calcutta. The latter shows little interest about the movement of the former. The registered shop keepers of Calcutta often criticise the street hawkers on the ground that the latter evade taxes which they pay regularly. The point to be noted is the registered small traders of Calcutta are no longer better off than the street hawkers.

The other section of the urban poor, especially the bus and taxi drivers also have a negative outlook towards the hawkers of Calcutta. They consider the latter socially inferior. They also resent as the latter create considerable nuisance to passing traffic. The city of Calcutta is yet to witness an organised or spontaneous movement amongst the participants of all street occupation like begging, hawking, vending, shoe shinning etc. "both socially and economically, the dominant links which affect street traders are vertical rather than horizontal and 'proletarian' or 'sub-proletarian' solidarity against elite interests is little more than a dream"[h].

Domination and Subordination

We have already pointed it out that there is a linkage between the formal and the informal sector where the former dominates always. This is one of the major causes, which makes the informal sector subservient to the former. For this reason, the dominant and subordinate relationship should be explored. But, before that, it would be prudent to analyse the process of transition, which will facilitate to understand such relationship.

The formal sector, as it is directed and regulated by the capitalist, may logically be considered as the capitalist sector. The latter destroys all elements of the pre-capitalist production and rectifies others according to its mode of operation. It is essential, therefore, to illustrate the ongoing process of dissolution-conservation as it characterizes all relation of production between the capitalist sector and the informal sector. The process of differentiation has two poles of transition, namely, proletarianization and movement in the reverse direction. The former is a process, which draws a portion of the informal petty producers, the 'unemployed' migrants into direct relationship, and capitalist mode of production while the latter can be clarified as an improving establishment of the capitalist system of production. Both the fringe are, however, supposed to be partial and affected by structural confinement in a sense that without an enormous employability of the capitalist sector, the informal petty producers can not become industrial wage earners en masse. The two poles of transition are articulated together and dependent on the strategies and actions of the capitalist sector and the reaction of the masses to their changing objective conditions.

The process of transformation from informal petty production to capitalist production (namely, the transformation of relation of personal dependence to those enabling surplus to be generated, appropriated and accumulated) emerges through an increment (i) in the level of employment, (ii) in the value of the means of production and (iii) in the stability in wage-employment. Among the informal petty procedures, differentiation can easily be noticed. The majority of such producers are having equipments of a very poor quality and narrow workshop while a few others acquire second hand machineries and equipped workshop. Very often, the expertise of this sector is not utilised properly. But, there is every sign that these producers are able to produce superior and profitable goods. The necessary condition for the evolution of an informal petty producer into a small capitalist manufacturer rests in the capacity for making the process of production more equipped and in the development of the relations of production commensurate with the accumulation of capital.

On the other hand, a static condition will prevail as long as the former will reproduce the same amount of capital with unaltered objective conditions of production.

But the evolutionary transformation for the informal petty producers is too difficult to achieve because most of the profitable or potential avenues have already been occupied and more practically monopolised by the capitalist sector. The minor avenues where the latter is yet to advent are those, which are still to be proved as 'profitable' for the capitalist production.

The informal petty producers have a predilection towards these minor avenues like property development, duplication of the prevailing production process, transport activities etc. These are the areas where both the 'have' and 'have nots' informal units owners intend to invest. Having a 'target' of this sort, how can such owners con make headway towards capital accumulation and under what conditions is this feasible?

Apart from this, a favourable transformation for the informal sectors producers towards small capitalist production requires the accessibility to bank or private credit facilities. In addition, there is the need to develop personal relations for the acquisition of credit and business orders. The search for the latter is in tune with the improvement in the level of technical and social relations of production which characterise such a transition wheres in the owners of the means of production undertake more and more responsibility of purchasing and marketing and gradually part himself with the mode of physical production. If wage-employment is so evolved, the production will be oriented towards the accumulation of wealth instead of mere reproduction. For the sake of progressive growth, the informal sector's producers must maintain and preserve a link with those from whom advantage and preference can be gained. Accordingly, there might be numerous transitional forms of production process. Instead of prescribing a typology of such transitional forms, in the following part we will illuminate the mechanism through which the informal petty producers are articulated with the dominant capitalist system.

Two Elucidative Cases

Two cases of articulation between the dominant and subordinate elements based on the Calcutta's metropolitan economy have been illustrated below. These will disclose the multiple mechanisms of exploitation at work. In addition to that, these will also highlight the twin poles of transition which affect the informal petty producers. These poles are, as mentioned already, the gradual development of capitalist relations of production and the concomitant process of proletarianization.

It is important to note that the persons, who are involved in the transition to capitalist accumulation and getting benefits as such, may not be always the producers of the informal sector. Although, it is undeniable that the productive operation of the latter acts as a focus of that transition. In many cases, the ability to start manufacturing activities informally has been gained through savings from past employment.

Even where the informal unit owners are enjoying real benefits in exchange of their labour to capital (although, it does not mean that they are advancing too far along the way to capitalist production) the labourers of such particular units are suffering from the limited exploitation by the owner of the means of production. They also suffer from additional exploitation (transmitted through their employer) for the sake of the benefits of string of capitalist subcontracts, bureaucrats, suppliers of raw materials etc. The latter are in the possession of commodities long before the entry of the labourers into the informal petty production process. This chain of exploitation can involve many diverse elements.

The capitalist mode of production by way of its commanding heights over the economy and by its mechanism to increase the labour's productivity through sophisticated tools and equipments not only obstructs the progressive growth of the informal sector but also imposes the burden of redundant labours which, in turn, swell the size of the labourers of the informal sector. The latter trend helps the capitalist sector to minimise long terms wage costs.

The government contract of commodities within the productive capacities of the informal sector's producers might be considered as a case for illustrating the tendency of the small capitalists. The latter occupies the midposition in between the actual producers of the informal sector and the ultimate customers. Such small capitalists or the contractors in particular, are having a possession of quasi monopoly of contracts and information regarding the public and private sector contracts irrespective of their considerable ignorance about the production process required to execute such contracts. These contractors utilise their accumulated wealth by procuring orders, contracts etc. which they then farm out to the petty producers of the informal sector. The latter, not being able to obtain the necessary license, is unacceptable either to the government or to the private sector.

The formation of cooperative amongst the informal petty producers of this sort might be a good solution as in that case, the latter would be able to secure the contracts directly in the name of the cooperative. It will also help them to share the actual remuneration, which would otherwise be appropriated by the contractors. The point to be noted is that the individual members of such cooperatives have often a little confidence in being able to compete successfully with the established contractors. On the contrary, they like to rely on securing smaller contracts individually from the latter. Thus, the petty producers of the informal sector "...are unable to benefit from state or other contracts in direct sense, their small-scale and consequent lack of economic 'muscle', their limited access to information and wide spatial dispersion permitting the rise of a new stratum of enterprising brokers".[i]

The surplus value created by the accumulation of wealth together with the effective personal contracts enriches the small capitalists without any actual involvement in the production process. Reverse is the case with the informal petty producers who undertake the total responsibility of absorbing many labourers for whom the capitalists have no liability. Still, the informal sector units are subject to high exploitation through the price system and through the legislated discrimination. This fact makes it clear that the capitalist sector appropriates the 'cream' (i.e. the struggle or the power of survival) of the informal sector. Yet, the limited success, the units owners of the latter sector achieve serve to keep them ideologically committed to individual perseverance.

Let us consider another case, which discloses the usual practice of sub contracting in the construction industry.

Besides, it explains how contractual relations might provide the mode of articulation between the capitalist accumulation and the gradual proletarianization of the indigenous workers. The construction companies whether foreign owned or indigenous act as the main contractors for building up housing complex and other construction jobs and provide few personnel at site. The entire work is then subcontracted to different independent contractors, some of whom complete the work themselves while others are, once again, subcontracting their portion of work to jobbing builders. The latter, like the subcontractors, either carry out the necessary work themselves using their own paid staff, apprentices and journeymen or again let it subcontracted to others.

This process of subcontracting allows the unproductive middlemen to appropriate the major portion of the contract value. But those who perform the work actually earn either a little (in the case of jobbing builders) or nothing at all (in the case of apprentices).

The chain of subcontracting also depicts that the major portion of cost which is deemed to accrue to the main contractors (i.e. the capitalist firms) is, in practice, borne by the lower tier (i.e., by the subcontractor of the subcontractor). It also supports the main contractor by reducing the total wage bills including perquisites to a countable labour force. However, in construction work, this is a common situation throughout the world still the picture of exploitation and appropriation is much clear in the context of developing countries due to abundant labour and scarce job opportunities.

The cases, mentioned above, illustrate the employment

linkage between the formal and the informal sector through subcontractual relations and the process of transferring value through the general price system. The informal sector's producers have a command only over his own labourers, the principal aspect of which is a domination over individuals as he can neither manipulate the input prices (other than labour) nor the market price of his product to any considerable extent. Therefore, the unit/owner of the informal sector is capable to regulate only the wage bills (for his own labour as well as for his subordinate workers). Nevertheless, with the resort of savings over a period of such wage-employment, some of the informal unit owners upgrade themselves to small capitalists. Thus, only to a very few informal petty producers, wage-employment for a number of years lets an opportunity of accelerating the volume of savings and useful contacts. These, in turn, have potential value to the individual embarking on self-employment.

The majority of the informal petty producers, however, consider their position unstable as their liquid fund is too short to stand against the intense competition. Unless a radical change takes place in every stratum of the economy of developing countries, considerable doubts can be expressed for the success of the majority of informal unit owners.

It is important, therefore, to explore into the problems of these non-industrially employed persons and then to prescribe policies accordingly.

Structure and Functioning of Labour Market in the Informal Sector

Any discussion relating to informal sector would not

have been completed if it does not consider the labour market of this sector. For an overall development of the informal sector, it is essential to know the structure and functioning of the labour market in such sector. This is also important for the purpose of policy making.

Within the urban economy of HOWRAH, the roles as found in the informal slum units in Nandy Bagan, adjacent to PILKHANA (one of the major slum areas of HOWRAH) are highly differentiated. To a great extent, these roles are related to caste or traditional occupation. Thus, role differentiation is concomitant with the imperfection of labour market.

The higher and the middle caste of the HINDUS, namely Brahmins, the Baidyas and the Kayastas, are generally carrying out such jobs as book binding, tailoring, embroidery and various types of designing, printing etc. The rural craftsman who settled here long ago has become goldsmiths, carpenters and brass vessel traders. Again, garland making, black smithy and bangle selling are also caste specific. The Muslims generally found in tailoring, biri binding or in shoe making. Traditional potters manufacture aluminum vessels, washer men set themselves in dry cleaning.

The lower castes as well as the harrijans (the untouchables) are noticed dealing in wines and have a special ability for chopping wood, removing coir from coconuts, cleaning sewers etc. Besides, they are also related to various arduous and virtually polluting tasks.

In the manufacturing industries particularly those related to the production of subsidiary engineering goods (mainly concentrated in the Belilious Road, Howrah) the Bengalis (a division of the Hindus) are the dominant class.

While in jute industries of Howrah, the major portion of labourers are the immigrants of Bihar, UP and Orissa. However, all these examples of traditional differentiation should not obscure the fact that caste by itself does not play a determining role in entry into the labour force of the informal sector.

The entry into the labour force of the informal units starts at a very early age with a few months' unpaid on-the-job-training, which could well be considered a test of such qualities as honesty and intelligence. It is followed by an apprenticeship at subsistence rates of wage.

The tenure of apprenticeship varies depending on the types of job. It takes three to five months to train a footpath tea stall waiter, four months for a helper of rag retailer's shop. Bicycle repairing takes on an average six months. Weighing, measuring, making paper cones and other related jobs of provision shops also take six months.

It takes at least one year to learn how to assess the value of jewel for the purpose of pawn broking while making jewellary as per design books takes some five to seven years, depending on age and perceptiveness. Learning how to manufacture wooden furniture takes about two years. The same period is also needed for learning how to mend pump sets and related machineries. To become an expert of power driven saw needs a training of about three years. Tailoring which includes diversified products (like frock, blouse, petty coat, shirts, trousers etc.) needs two to three years training.

However, it is difficult to determine whether within the informal sector the apprenticeship period is longer in trade or in manufacturing. This is because this sector is characterised by countless activities. Nevertheless, it can be said that this sector transmits skill through the supply of trained employees.

There exists occupational rigidity for the workers other than those who are employed in the electricals or in the petty engineering units. At the end of apprenticeship, a considerable portion of the employees try to accumulate capital for being established as independent unit owners. Only a few of them can fulfill their mission. Such employees are characterised by a high degree of indetedness to their employers. The use of incentives to attract desirably 'trained' employees is confined to indebtedness. It may be considered as exploitative since as found in many cases, indebtedness is the cause behind the stability of labour force. According to Scott. "Objectively measured levels of exploitation, if it is possible to calculate them, may not be recognised as such by participants who have their own criteria of injustice"[(j)].

There exists precise division of labour in almost all types of informal units established in Nandy Bagan. In addition, there are several forms of organisation of labour. For example, horizontal organisation can be marked amongst those who mainly depend on brawn or amongst the owners of capital and skill. But such example is rare amongst the 'apprentices' who are interested only in accumulating capital, if possible by currying favour with an employer, or are vertically cemented by debt.

The entry to the gang of urban collies is restricted by the recommendation from a member, caste or village of origin. Comparatively few harijans (untouchables) are allowed to enter into such gang. Each gang operates in a particular territory with separate gangman who distributes works, earnings and negotiates piece rates. Truly proletariat are engaged in garbage picking, begging, sifting sewage and waste from ditches in search of any article, starting from junk, rubber to even 'gold dust' which might have some resale value. Sometimes, they also manage casual work in the informal slum units of Nandy Bagan or Pilkhana.

Organisation of the owners of capital reflects various types of interest and activity. As found in some cases, petty producers of the informal sector group themselves by commodity. The raison d'etra of these groups is only to protect their own interest particularly when their livelihood is threatened.

These groups have, therefore, a little economic significance.

So, there is clear evidence for specification of roles and for organisation of labour. It is also difficult to disentangle caste from technical qualification because occupations and skill are too much caste specific. Since allocation of job to a particular caste does not indicate that the members of the caste have no technical qualification. Again, there are many employers who are not interested in technical qualification because they are to provide the recipient with them in exchange of a formal education, the cost of which can not be afforded by the latter's family.

One point should be emphasized here. Lack of formal qualification does not stand for lack of intelligence, skill or aptitude. The informal sector does not play the role of absorptive buffer[(k)]. On the contrary, it chooses its workers in a way similar to that of formal sector. As the level of education is poor, personal recommendation, family background etc. play a key role for establishing suitability. It is to be noted that as an entry criteria these are almost universally accepted. The contractual relation is based on 'training' on the supply side and on 'wage rate' on the demand side. Generally speaking, it is not at all related to caste or to village of origin. Examples of such relation are most common in the informal units producing paper packet or plaster doll where both the employers and the employees come from a variety of castes and in the repairing job where even the untouchables have broken into the trade. Therefore, the informal sector may be considered as organized to some extent because of the existence of order, rule and structure within it, which keep a good pace with Weber's organizational norm.

In order to outline the extent of adherence to Weber's organizational norm in the informal sector, the lack of differentiation between household and business in the latter sector should be enlightened. Most of the petty producers of the informal sector live within the business premises and cannot separate production cost from consumption cost.

In true sense, there is evidence of 'formal' behaviour in the informal sector as well as of 'informal' behaviour in the formal sector. To differentiate labour market by this dichotomy is, therefore, counter productive. Since both 'informal' and 'formal' sector is nothing but parts of a whole economic activities. The government of India defines and classifies the informal sector as arbitrarily as it is done by many other governments of the third world. The observance of the necessary regulations is perhaps more costly than is the provision of welfare in the informal sector. The latter is supposed to be afforded by the unit owner of the informal sector. The existence of the latter acts as a brake on industrial expansion so that it may pay an industrialist to diversify and remain under the threshold of the formal sector rather than to evolve and merge into that sector.

In practical field, there are several strata of industrial activities in terms of volume. Many people move between the two sectors at different parts of their life span. In fact, the informal sector acts as a springboard for the formal sector for young men up to the upper age limit after that it becomes a trap. Of course, this interpretation may not always come true as the informal sector, in some market town, contributes to a large extent in the urban economy. Nevertheless, some people have a dream to start their own business units after retirement and many would like to start trading activities but do not dare. In course of our field study, we have been informed that some of the inhabitants of the Nandy Bagan have fulfilled their dream: one, who had retired from engineering units of Howrah, has started to produce electrical goods with his life time savings. Another person who was formerly employed in a merchant firm of Calcutta has set up a provisions shop.

In addition, we should also consider that countable person who move to the informal sector from agriculture and return back when monsoon appears in the traditional sector (as we find in the case of tanneries). It is evidenced that both sectors contain people related in various ways both to the means of production and circulation.

Conclusion

The informal sector exists in the structural opposition

to the formal sector, though it may not be traceable from official records. In relation to the formal sector, the informal sector may also exist in the marginal pole or in a specific context. Therefore, for the purpose of analysis, the labour market of the informal sector has a little internal variability than cross category variability.

The production system of the informal sector is trapped in an involutionary impasse and consequently it could reproduce only it's conditions of survival, mostly at the cost of it's own standard of living and labour remuneration. The excessive influx of migrated labour to urban sector along with the existing urban jobless people imposes responsibility for providing employment, which falls squarely on the petty producers of the informal sector. Under such condition, impoverishment of the masses is inevitable.

Each generation of the informal petty producers that undergoes this insidious marginalisation suffers from a loss in terms of their accumulated skills. Still, in the underdeveloped countries, it is a part of the overall problem relating to the evolution of self-reliant and equitable development. The future of the mass people depends on that of the informal petty production and if no action being taken to enable them to participate fully in the process of national social development, the future of these people appears bleak. In fact, the real problem is how to bring harness between the plentiful human resources and material prerequisites in the task of development. Yet, the masses are off the main track, exploited and tied to individualistic ideologies, which are reproduced by the environment in which, economic and social life is deeply rooted. Both the structure and the orientation of the underdeveloped economy should be transformed radically before all exploited sections of the masses can benefit from equitable and equal participation.

But, the notable point is, in a particular situation, informal units are able to compete with the modern units irrespective of several obstacles. This is due to the imperfection of markets, which we have already enumerated. In this special case, informal trading activities within the overall framework of job scarcity in the modern units represent an efficient use of resources. Nevertheless, this achievement is not enough to anticipate any trend for the long run and hence the rhythm is difficult to forecast. We could only remark that the ability of the petty producers of informal sector to compete will ensure their survival.

However, the inter-relationship between the formal and the informal sector should be explored further. This may raise several questions like whether the ability to compete results in a surplus which, in turn, generates a rapid diffusion of informal units or whether concentration hinders their expansion allowing only to survive and not to grow? So far as our field experience is considered, the latter is true in many cases. Yet it requires more explanation before drawing any conclusion in this regard.

In addition, it is also necessary to overhaul further whether demand segmentation prevails in the sense that low income household prefer to buy more labour intensive products generally manufactured by the informal units. The required study may be based on such areas other than the area considered by us in this chapter. It is of profound importance for the purpose of generalization. These are, therefore, some of the tentative issues on which further study is most welcome.

REFERENCES

(a) Street traders of Calcutta are a good case for example. There exist conflicts of interest between such street traders. This particular occupation is highly competitive with numerous hawkers forcing the margins down. This 'little' margin is obtained by selling the products at a price less than that of shop or super market and by carrying out the work for long hours and over a wider range of location.

(b) V.E. Tokman: "Competition between the informal and formal sectors in retailing: The case of SANTIAGO" found in the Urban Informal Sector: ed. by R. Bromely, pp. 1188-1197.

(c) D. Sansone: Technologia Y Empleo en Servicios: El Caso del Comercio minorista de Alimentos en chile (Santiago: PRELAC: 77).

(d) V.E. Tokman, *ibid.*

(e) Being practically nil in the case of suger, detergent, tea and soaps, as the study disclosed. Besides according to this study, there are a few products like flour, spaghetti etc., which are sold at a lower price in the informal units than in the modern units.

(f) Besides, one may also count the political organisation of the small traders of informal sector as a non-economic reason behind the survival of this sector. Sharing experience with the street trading of Calcutta, it can be realized that any attempt to eliminate such traders will act as a direct threat to the interest of the industrialists, middlemen and moneylenders. It is doubtful how far the elite group of Calcutta will all agree upon the elimination of street hawkers due to their vested interest.

(g) V.E. Tokman, *ibid.*, p. 1196.

(g_1) These are: Bengal Hawkers Association, Calcutta street Hawkers Samiti and United Hawkers. The first one is the oldest and it was formed in the early '50's with the strong support of the refugees of former East Pakistan (Now Bangladesh). It is affiliated to T.U.C.C. of Forward Block. At present, Calcutta Street Hawkers Samiti has the largest members. It is affiliated to C.I.T.U. of Communist Party of India (Marxist). United Hawkers was formed in the late '60's and it is affiliated to I.N.T.U.C. of Congress(I).

(h) R. Bromely: "Organisation, regulation and exploitation in the so called 'urban informal sector': The street traders of CALI, Columbia" in the Urban Informal Sector: ed. by R. Bromley, p. 1168.

(i) Chris Gerry: "Petty production and capitalist production in Dakar: The crisis of self-employed" found in 'The Urban Informal Sector' ed. by R. Bromley, p. 1156.

(j) J. Scott: "Exploitation in Rural Class Relations": Comparative Politics: Vol. 7. ('75), pp. 490-532.

(k) J. K. Hart (1973), J. Breman (1976a).

6

Employment Potential of the Informal Sector*

One of the obvious reasons for the rapid diffusion of the urban informal sector in the developing countries is the implementation of massive urbanization programme without a balanced policy of industrialization. In this chapter, we are concerned with the employment potential of the informal sector which starts with the disclosure of present volume of employment of the urban informal sector including some notable points which are based on several study reports concerning this sector.

Next we have explored into the nature of informal sector in order to know whether this sector is characterized by an autonomous capacity for improving the incomes of the urban poor. In this context, we have highlighted different study reports of the practitioners.

Thereafter, the determinants of employment potential of the informal sector have been identified and analysed in an input-output framework. As evident in our model, the crucial variables, which, in conjunction with the elasticity of employment with respect to output in the informal sector, determine the employment potential, are:

An abstract of the core portion of this chapter was published as a doctoral dissertation paper in Finance India (New Delhi, India) vol. XI, No. 1, March 1997, pp. 99-104.

Interested readers may also see : Utpal Chowdhury (1996) " The Informal Sector : conceptual framework, employment potential and scheme for amelioration" in Artha Beekshan (Calcutta, India) Vol. 5, No. 1, June 1996, pp. 91-106.

(i) Changes in aggregate income, (ii) Changes in the relative price levels, (iii) technical change and (iv) changes in consumer tastes.

The expatiation of the mathematical model clearly indicates that several advantages can be derived if there is an evolutionary growth of the informal sector. It also discloses the types of changes which affect the informal sector.

In the conclusion, we have stressed on the need for the formulation of policies for tapping the employment potential of the informal sector.

Preamble

In the developing countries, planning for urbanization has not been matched properly with industrialization. This, in turn, creates a space for the growth of informal sector whose behaviour is induced by the modern sector. The growing urban labourers (more practically, the 'victims' of massive urbanization without industrialization) are being absorbed in the informal sector increasingly. The agglomeration of economically productive urban populace in this sector has already been enlightened in different studies. The informal sector has been demarcated as a sector where among other features (i) labour market is flexible in terms of wages and supply of labour and (ii) the use of overhead imposes minimum burden on the prevailing social infrastructure.

In fact, there is a diversity of opinion among the researchers, which make it difficult to relate the broad contours of the informal sector. " ...... detailed analysis of the sector is, however, handicapped by lack of not only data but also standard definitions and measurement techniques[(aa)]". In addition, a problem arises when we are to define such people who are not regarded under the conventional categories as employed though they are working at economically viable and rewarding jobs. From a group of such works which may be considered as informal, the term informal employment may include the self employed, proletariat and even those who support themselves but yet are not considered as vagrants.

However, the data available in this regard will exhibit a picture about the percentage of urban labour force engaged in the informal sector of some of the developing countries. This is represented in the Table 1.21.

It is evident from the table that the informal sector is equipped with employment potential. Perhaps, this is the reason why does this sector become more viable as economic entities. In the prevailing circumstances in India, it is doubtful whether large-scale industries or agricultural sector could solve the problem of unemployment. As there is the scarcity of capital and plethora of labour, it would be prudent to emphasize on the capital light industries which might play due role in creating additional job opportunities.

In a recent survey in Bangkok[g], it was found that 70% of the workers of the informal sector are unskilled and over 60% of them come from rural areas. Analysing their gender division, it has been marked that male workers are concentrated in such fields as construction, tailoring and transport while the female workers predominate in the small trading and service activities. In Thailand, percentage of women engaged in the informal sector is more than that of male workers. This fact does not keep pace with the informal sector of other countries where male workers predominate. Other relevant features disclosed by the above study are: workers are paid at piece rate and non-existence of fixed working hours especially for the self-employed persons.

TABLE 1.21

Selected Economies in the ESCAP Region

Name of the country	*City/District*	*%age of urban labour force employed in the informal sector*	
Bangladesh[(a)]		50	
	Dhaka (1981)[(b)]		65
India[(ac)]		44-75	
	Ahmedabad (1971)[(c)]		46.5
	Bombay (1971)[(c)]		39.5-50.4
	Calcutta (1971)[(d)]		40-50
	Delhi (1971)[(c)]		53.8
	Madras (1971)[(c)]		50-70
	Valsad (1977)[(c)]		75
Indonesia[(e)]		54	
	Jakarta (1976)[(d)]		45
Malaysia		Not available	
	Urban areas of West Malaysia (1970) [(d)]		35
Pakistan (1972)[(d)]		69	
Singapore (1970) [(d)]		23	
Sri Lanka[(a)]		23	
	Colombo (1971) [(d)]		19
Thailand (1976) [(d)]		26	
	Bangkok (1981) [(f)]		87

In Bangladesh[(h)], the workers of informal sector work, in most cases, for all the days of a week. The working hours is as long as twelve hours while the earning of 59% of workers is as low as $ 30 p.m. i.e. the average wage of the country as a whole. In this context, it is not irrelevant to note that in Calcutta, the average wage of the workers of informal sector is less than $ 20 p.m. and that of Bangkok is $ 80 p.m.

The above facts about the informal sector may not be encouraging. But what is important to note that this sector provides a source of sustenance to a considerable portion of urban labour force in may developing countries, which the formal sector fails to provide. Informal sector has been viewed as a new growth pole, an island of development and an effective training school for larger industry. In addition, the petty producers of the informal sector also constitute a sizeable proportion of the urban economically active population[(i)]. In this regard, one might encounter the relationship of a city with the urban system as a determinant of the induced labour demand in the informal sector.

As there is the existence of two distinct sectors in the developing country's economy, namely formal and informal, we should search for the growth potential of the latter in the terms dictated by the former. This is because the former dominates the latter. In broad sense, such terms may be within the scale of production or in the technological progress.

In the ESCAP region, many governments have adopted some ameliorative programmes and policy measures for an improvement of the informal sector. These include provision of infrastructure, stemming the rural – urban exodus by launching development in the former area,[(j)] providing vocational training programmes, promoting the production and sales co-operatives and improving the credit system in order to minimize the obstacles for sanctioning loan to informal sector.[(k)]

Of these, the effect of social infrastructure investment on the urban poverty levels should be considered with due importance. Since, it creates not only direct employment but also provides an additional source of real income to the urban poor by the development of housing, health and education.

In addition to the above, the respective authority of some of the developing countries also provides contracts to the petty producers for supplying such commodities, which are required by various government departments as the existing rules of those countries militate against them for being accepted as a contractor. However, the government should be more cautious least the beneficiaries (i.e. the petty producers) can not utilize their accumulated wealth to act as a contract brokers.

Off the Track

The point to be highlighted is the informal sector causes due concern in the government level. There is every sign to encourage the evolution of this sector by the state authorities. It discloses that there it a trend to appreciate a basic fact that the unmarked, unaided petty producers of the informal sector can progress. The problems related to the development of this sector are considered as being remedial through some promotional schemes as mentioned above.

The aggregate results of such schemes have been misunderstood as the analysis of different projects have been based upon a pragmatic, disjointed and essentially dualistic conception of economy. In this regard, the state must determine the most efficient allocation of its available resource. The initial question, which should be asked and answered, is: whether it distributes the total promotion budget equally among a large number of informal unit owners or ameliorate them selectively? The state's preoccupation with the success of promoted units may require partial treatment which will undoubtedly affect those units not benefited from promotion. Similarly, an open economy might inspire, by virtue of promotion, predatory attacks by the successful enterprises whose strategies are not limited by small budget.

The Nature of the Informal Sector

Eyeing the employability of the informal sector, the question arises inevitably whether the labourers of the informal sector represent a passive, exploited majority or whether their activities pose an autonomous power for improving the level of income of the urban poor?

In order to answer it, an exploration into the process of accumulation is required. This will, in turn, enlighten the nature of the informal sector. "Informal sector activities generate surplus or can do it provided that the policy environment does not discriminate against them[l]". Hart ('70 and '73) and ILO('72) observed that the informal sector is characterized by the potential of growth with a more egalitarian distribution of income. A sizeable portion of labour force gets an opportunity within the informal sector to produce or sell something, which generates income. These labourers would otherwise swell the rank of unemployment. "Their ingenuity to make a living out of a situation of lack of access to resources and to markets and their capacity of survival under unfavourable conditions proof that they have the potential for further developing their activities[m]." The growth potential of this sector has been marked as autonomous and the informal sector, itself, has been defined as a self-contained segment of the economy (ILO '72, Oshima '71, Sethu Raman '75). Oshima[n] ('71) pointed out "Proprietors and their family help and employees work for each other and buy each other's products". In fact, the autonomous informal sector is more efficient and comparatively advantageous if we consider such activities, which are developed, in both formal and informal sector. "It's main advantage is the socially adequate factor proportions used in the process of production, since labour is used at a maximum without exerting heavy pressures on capital or on foreign exchange"[o]. In addition to this, there is the use of second hand machinery and indigenous technology, which help to minimize the new capital requirements. This does not indicate inefficiency because there are a variety of activities in the informal sector performed with a very little capital cost even with an upgrading of techniques. The most efficient use of the prime components creates a surplus, which, if properly reinvested, can foster further growth. Individual savings of the persons within the informal sector are too low[p] and spent mostly for durable goods, house improvements and new constructions. Frankenhoff ('67) cited an example of capital formation in housing in favela communities of Riode Janeiro which disclosed that the value of capital formation reached at a significant level and that the rehabilitation of that community constitute an economically more feasible alternative than their abolishment. The growth potential of the informal sector gets a momentum when it is articulated to the rest of the economy.

Hart ('73) pointed out that the informal sector is mainly the exporter of different products and services, specifically, the illegitimate services. In the circulation process, this sector plays an important role due to its easy accessibility to the customers. Besides, the provision of credit and selling in as small units as required should also be counted in this respect. Informal sector, as viewed by him, if properly managed, could offer means to generate independent and development oriented industrialisation.

According to Mc Gee ('73), the traders of informal sector are engaged in vertical exchange of commodities,- both upward and down ward. He argued that it would be upward vertical exchange when such traders are selling foodstuffs to the urban poor. But, it would be down ward vertical exchange when they deal in urban produced goods like textiles.

As pointed out by Hart ('70), informal sector provides important service in transport and communication in such developing countries where these basic services are not sufficient. Webb ('74) marked that the informal sector is highly integrated to the rest of the economy. Three-fourth of the total production of this sector is being exported while a similar proportion is being imported to this sector for consumption. Such an articulation is fruitful since the export is service oriented – related either to commerce or household – which is complementary to the production of the formal sector. The growth potential of the informal sector is accelerated by it's access through these traders which finally inroad into the expanding markets of the rest of the economy. For this reason, it has become a realized fact that this sector has a growth potential whether autonomous or integrated. In addition, this growth may be considered evolutionary since an increasing number of labourers can be absorbed at higher average income.

The latter part has been elaborated by Week ('73). He maintains that the growth of informal sector is beyond doubt; therefore, in his opinion, the relevant question is whether this growth is involutionary or evolutionary. In the former case, a large number of working masses are incorporated at a stagnant or diminishing level of real income. While in the latter case, such absorption is at an incremental wage rate.

Another point to be noted is the rate of expansion of the informal sector depends neither on the growth of the formal sector nor on the increased supply of labour. However, with several types of growth in both formal and informal sector, it is probable that average income and productivity will remain constant while employment grows rapidly in the informal sector. Moreover, the growth rate of formal and informal sector is likely to be the same provided consumer's preference for the informal sector goods remains stable.

The economic surplus of the informal sector is transferred to the rest of the economy. This may be viewed as an intermediate step of the transfer of surplus from periphery to centre. Although the mechanism through which surplus is transferred from this sector takes a variety of shape. For example, the working masses of the informal sector receive poor wages. This, in turn, enlarges the surplus value, which is transferred to the formal sector through financial mechanism. It is not irrelevant to point out in this context that the demand for the products of the informal sector is limited owing to its marked subordination.

In the yardstick like transfer of surplus, it is beyond question that there is a significant link between the informal sector and the rest of the economy. Different studies make it clear that in a competitive framework, the growth potential of the informal sector is higher specially when the related activities of this sector are already well advanced[q].

In order to depict the growth potential product wise classification (for example, manufactured goods, personal services, distributory services, financial services etc.) of the informal sector activities is justified. However, it would be imprudent to expect a permanent expansion of those informal activities, which are being operated in oligopolistic condition. Because, the evolution of such activities pass through continuum where expansion or contraction depend solely on the trend of demand, minimum scale of operation, economies of scale etc. They could benefit from short-term profits but in the long period they might have to lose markets which is, in fact, a case of most of the informal manufacturing activities. Of course, this does not mean that the informal activities operating under the condition of oligopoly will be abolished, or that they will steadily decline, as the prevailing factors might create a less pronounced trend or even a reverse one. For example, factors like clientele relations, location and minimum size of sale favour the informal sector along with the predominant family labour, which makes wages more flexible and lets a space for evasion of official regulations.

However, an evolution is possible for those informal activities, which are not under oligopoly market. As found in many developing countries, such a possibility is marked with the informal units producing shoes.

Although technical change in the informal activities relating to personal services is more gradual but their existence in an economy with higher level of income is sufficient for presuming their expansion. However, such an expansion may not be rapid due to their low-income elasticity. There is also the possibility of "unequal exchange" which might develop against the service workers especially when other activities do not transfer the benefits of productivity gains to prices.

For informal commerce activities, a trend to oligopolisation seems unlikely and there is a gradual change in technology. Such activities might survive for long period due to market imperfection, particularly, the demand behaviour at low-income levels. The latter induces product differentiation, which, in turn, makes a room for permanency of this sort of activities. In addition, these activities could enjoy a share in the overall market due to such factors as infinite product subdivision, limitless business hours, owner – customer relationship etc.

A recent phenomenon of the less developed countries, as disclosed by the official surveys concerning employment is that a mild growth of employment has been accompanied by a rapid growth of output. This is simply because a large number of wage earners of the informal sector are not counted in official surveys. As a consequence, there is a tendency to swell the level of urban unemployment.

The fact that the informal sector could provide mass employment has already been mentioned. What we are yet to describe is the determinants of growth of output and employment in the urban informal sector of the less developed countries[r]. For this purpose, we exhibit below an analytical framework in order to describe the interaction between formal and informal sector of the non-agricultural economic activities in the less developed countries.

The Mathematical Model

The determinants of the employment potential i.e., the

growth of employment in the informal sector can be organized in an input-output framework. Our model has four sectors[(s)]. Peasant agriculture (sector 1), the informal sector (sector 2), the private formal sector (sector 3) and the government sector (sector 4).

The outputs of the sectors are X_1, X_2, X_3, X_4 and the final demands Y_1, Y_2, Y_3, Y_4 where these are for peasant agriculture, informal sector, formal sector and government sector respectively.

In order to provide an analytical tool, we have arranged the above assumptions in an input-output flow table in the following way :

TABLE 1.22

Four Sector Input-Output Model

Sectors	*Inputs to Sector 1*	*Inputs to Sector 2*	*Inputs to Sector 3*	*Inputs to Sector 4*	*Final Demands*	*Total Outputs*
1	$a_{11}X_1$	$a_{12}X_2$	$a_{13}X_3$	$a_{14}X_4$	Y_1	X_1
2	$a_{21}X_1$	$a_{22}X_2$	$a_{23}X_3$	$a_{24}X_4$	Y_2	X_2
3	$a_{31}X_1$	$a_{32}X_2$	$a_{33}X_3$	$a_{34}X_4$	Y_3	X_3
4	$a_{41}X_1$	$a_{42}X_2$	$a_{43}X_3$	$a_{44}X_4$	Y_4	X_4
Labour Services	X_{01}	X_{02}	X_{03}	X_{04}	—	—

Notes

(1) a_{11}, a_{12}, a_{13} etc are the input coefficient; (2) $a_{11}X_1$ indicates amount of X_1 going as input to X_1. Similarly, $a_{21}X_1$ indicates amount of X_2 going to X_1 as an input and so for others; (3) The FINAL DEMANDS column shows the commodity breakdown of what is available for consumption; (4) Each column, thought of as a whole (i.e. as a VECTOR) represents the input (or cost) structure of the respective sectors; (5) Each row shows the allocation of total output of the respective sectors; (6) We make the convention that

labour is not directly consumed. It is coming form outside at an exogenously given rate. Let X_0=total labour supply = $X_{01}+X_{02}+X_{03}+X_{04}$.

The total output of different sectors, as evident in the above table, is exhausted according to the following identity:

$$X_1 = a_{11}X_1+a_{12}X_2+a_{13}X_3+a_{14}X_4+Y_1$$
$$X_2 = a_{21}X_1+a_{22}X_2+a_{23}X_3+a_{24}X_4+Y_2$$
$$X_3 = a_{31}X_1+a_{32}X_2+a_{33}X_3+a_{34}X_4+Y_3$$
$$X_4 = a_{41}X_1+a_{42}X_2+a_{43}X_3+a_{44}X_4+Y_4$$

Let us arrange the above in the form of matrix :

$$\begin{bmatrix} X_1 \\ X_2 \\ X_3 \\ X_4 \end{bmatrix} = \begin{bmatrix} a_{11} & a_{12} & a_{13} & a_{14} \\ a_{21} & a_{22} & a_{23} & a_{24} \\ a_{31} & a_{32} & a_{33} & a_{34} \\ a_{41} & a_{42} & a_{43} & a_{44} \end{bmatrix} \begin{bmatrix} X_1 \\ X_2 \\ X_3 \\ X_4 \end{bmatrix} + \begin{bmatrix} Y_1 \\ Y_2 \\ Y_3 \\ Y_4 \end{bmatrix}$$

Note : $a_{11,}$ $a_{12,}$ a_{13} etc, are the technical coefficients of A. With the help of the above matrix, the relationship between the use of inputs, final outputs and final demands can be expressed as :

(1) $X = AX + R$

Where X = vector of gross output, A = matrix of technical coefficients and R = vector of final demands.

Equation (1) can be written as : $X - AX = R$ or, $(I - A) X=R$.

Pre-multiplying both sides of $(I - A)X=R$ by $(I - A)^{-1}$ we get,

(2) $X = (I - A)^{-1}R$.

It is to be noted here that the following technical coefficients are not needed at all for the informal sector (i.e. sector 2) and, therefore, these are assumed to be zero : $-a_{31}$, $-a_{41}$, $-a_{42}$ and $-a_{14}$

After finding $(I - A)^{-1}$, we can solve for the gross outputs $(X_1.......X_4)$ in terms of the final demands. X_2 can be written as follows :

$$(3)\quad X_2 = {}^1/_b\,[a_{21}\,Y_1 + (1-a_{11})Y_2 + g_1\,(a_{23}, a_{24}, M_1)\,Y_3 + g_2\,(a_{23}, a_{24}, M_2)\,Y_4]$$

where the functions g_1 and g_2 are coefficients which are a function of various technical coefficients, a_{23},a_{24} and the remaining ones aggregated within M_1.

The final demands of the sectors are given by the following functions :

$$(4)\quad Y_1 = Y_1\,(Z)$$

Where Z=aggregate income.

$$(5)\quad Y_2 = Y_2\,(Z,P,Q)$$

Where P = ratio of the price level in sector 2 to that in sector 3 and Q = consumer taste parameter.

$$(6)\quad Y_3 = Y_3\,(Z,P,Q)$$

$$(7)\quad Y_4 = Y_4\,(p,Z)$$

Where P = Population.

We make three simplifying assumptions : (i) the price levels in sector 1 and 4 are constant, (ii) there is substitution between products for sector 2 and 3 only; and (iii) changes in consumer tastes affect the distribution of final demands between sector 2 and 3 only. Further, for policy purposes, the imput coefficients should not be treated as constant over time. For current purposes, we are interested in the intermediate demands for sector 2, the informal sector. We are particularly interested in the intermediate demands by the formal sector and government, which, can be affected by government policy. Assuming production costs constant(t), the technical coefficients are determined by technological change :

$$(8)\quad a_{23} = a_{23}\,(T)$$

Where T = technological shift parameter.

$$(9)\quad a_{24} = a_{24}(T)$$

We now substitute expressions (4) to (9) into the expression for total output. Assuming all technical coefficients except a_{23} and a_{24} to be constant, or that all others change in a compensating manner (so that $dM_i = O$). We take the total derivative of X_2. This equation is rendered an expression for employment growth by substituting :

$X_2 = 1_2 L_2$.

Where 1_2 = marginal output labour ratio in sector 2.

In the short run, if population is constant, we get :

$$(10)\quad L'_2 = dL_2/L_2 = E/X_2 b$$

$$\{(a_{21}\,\partial Y_1/\partial Z + (1-a_{11})\,\partial Y_2/\partial Z + g_1\,\partial Y_3/\partial Z + + g_2\,\partial Y_4/\partial Z\}dZ$$

$$+ \{(1-a_{11})\,\partial Y_2/\partial P + g_1\,\partial Y_3/\partial P\}dP$$

$$+ \partial a_{23}/\partial T(\partial g_1/\partial a_{23} Y3 + \partial g_2/\partial a_{23} Y_4)\,dT + \partial a_{24}/\partial T(\partial g_1/\partial a_{24} Y_3 + \partial g_2/\partial a_{24} Y_4)dt$$

$$+ \{(1-a_{11})\,\partial Y_2/\partial Q + g_1\,\partial Y_3/\partial Q\}dQ$$

The four lines in expression (10) of the model can be expressed as follows moving from top to bottom : the induced and final demand effect on employment (dZ); the relative price change effect on employment, i.e., the change in the ratio of price level in the informal sector to the price level in the formal sector (dP), it is being assumed in the model that the price levels in the two other sectors are constant; the technological effect on employment (dT); and the consumer taste effect on employment (dQ). Thus, the crucial variables in determining the growth of informal sector demand are (i) the changes in aggregate income, (ii) changes in the relative price levels, (iii) technical change and (iv) changes in consumer tastes. It is these variables which, in conjunction with the elasticity of employment with respect to output in the informal sector (Sector 2) determine the employment potential i.e. the growth of employment in that Sector (L'_2).

An Interpretation of the Mathematical Model

From expression (10) of the mathematical model we could frame out policies for an evolutionary growth in the informal sector (Sector 2). The advantages of such a growth in a developing country are:

Firstly : as the informal sector provides a supply of significant portion of consumer goods for the lower income group, an expansion of this sector will reduce the dependency on import "reproduction" [u] which due to the dependence on foreign technology contributes a little to employment expansion.

Secondly : the workshops of the informal sector provide the source of a local capital goods industry as well as an apprenticeship for the indigenous entrepreneurs.

Thirdly : the growth of informal sector will induce a labour-intensive form of industrialization which, will increase employment/output ratio and ensure an efficient utilization of capital.

The above expression of the mathematical model also discloses the sorts of change that affect the informal sector.

Firstly: considering changes in aggregate demand, it is evident that the upward shift in aggregate income (Z) will have a large effect on the rate of growth of employment in the informal sector(L'_2). Other things remaining unchanged, the higher the rate of induced and final demand effect on employment (dZ), the greater will be the rate of growth of employment in the informal sector (L'_2). The component of final and intermediate output for a given dZ depends on the distribution of income. Other than household service, worker of the informal sector produces such goods and services as cater to the taste of lower income groups. Hence, a maldistribution of income keeps the final and intermediate demand apart from the informal sector. This indicates that in course of time demand will change towards less labour intensive production system.

Therefore, such a policy should be framed as could shift the final demand towards the informal sector in order to generate an equal distribution of income through it's employment promoting effect.

In the above context, government purchases of goods and services from the informal sector have a positive role to play. This might cause for a shift in the level of private final demand towards the informal sector that, in turn, results in less capital and import intensive public demand. This is inevitable because of the complementarity between private and public demand.

However, the potentiality lies in firming out orders to informal sectors is not realized because of excessive and irrelevant 'quality' requirements. Nevertheless, it is possible to trace out the following as changeable from capital – intensive to labour – intensive suppliers such as construction, clothing, furniture, printing, maintenance etc. It is beyond doubt that to monitor the small manufacturers is much difficult than large expatriate producers. But, in course of time, it would be a less serious problem than that of a growing surplus labour of the urban areas.

Considering the first line of expression (10) in the mathematical model, it is clear that the promotion of employment in the informal sector is complementary with an emphasis on agricultural improvement. For a country where " .... The agricultural sector is predominantly small holder, pouring development expenditure into agriculture will stimulate small-scale rural non-agricultural activity as a by product".[v] The informal sector (Sector 2) could provide ordinary agricultural tools and the processing (For example : Grain milling, tobacco – drying, saw milling, brick making and other less important types of processing) and transportation. This indicates the facilities that could be obtained from the informal sector (Sector 2) industrialization for assisting the peasant agriculture (Sector 1). It can be said, therefore, the expansion of the informal sector is complementary with the growth of the peasant agriculture. The second line of expression (10) in the mathematical model clearly depicts that raising of wages in the formal sector may lead to price-rise of sector 3 output and as a consequence there might be product substitution between sectors 2 and 3. Another point that has not been considered is the effect of increased wages in sector 3 on the level of demand. If the wage increases relative to other factor shares and the preference of wage earners for consuming sector 2 products is greater than that of group whose income increases more slowly, the output of informal sector (Sector 2) will raise proportionately to any given change in final demand.

The nature and pace of technical change determines the degree of relation between the informal sector and the private formal and government sectors. Again, technical change, itself, is a function of choice of products. Due to the operation of sophisticated technology for quality reason the private formal sector cannot provide sufficient opportunity for subcontracting or for primary inputs supplied by the small producers. Through proper distribution of income, such a situation can be altered indirectly. Since the common tendency of the lower income groups is to consume labour-intensive basket of goods.

Another remedial method for redressing factor price imbalances which encourage capital intensity might be to eliminate the duty-free access to machinery, accelerated depreciation rebates etc, and to allocate more resources on research which, in turn, will innovate the techniques and equipments most suitable for the small enterprise[w].

The countries which are seriously suffering from unemployment problem should offer condition to the foreign investors that their investment plans would be allowed to implement only when it includes definite proposals for small-scale subcontracting including industrial expansion and training services.

The above measures have a possible effect for changing the values of the technological parameters. In fact, in most of the underdeveloped countries, the tendency to change technology in favour of large-scale formal sector is not inherent but the consequence of improper distribution of income institutionally administered input prices and favourable terms and conditions for the foreign investors. "To the extent that large, capital-intensive enterprises are technically more efficient, this is the consequence not of the inexorable march of technology but of the fact that most industrial research and development is conducted in labour-scarce economies".[x]

One recent feature of the underdeveloped countries is to replace indigenous products by standardised, mass-produced consumer goods. (For example, plastic sandals, bread, could drinks, soap etc.). These products have a wide market and the consumption of these products might well increase with a more equal distribution of income. There is nothing inexorable for the substitution of these products.

In this regard, one should trace out the reasons of the customer's choice. There might be four reasons[y] behind such preference :

1. The mass produced products are manufactured in a technically more efficient manner and would be cheaper at any wage/profit ratio.
2. The mass produced products are cheaper only at existing wage and profit rates and capital is under valued in the market.
3. While no cheaper, firms making monopolistic profits that can afford extensive advertising outlays beyond the resources of informal sector enterprises produce the products.
4. Consumers in less developed countries genuinely prefer formal sector products independently of advertising and propaganda even if informal sector products are cheaper.

From the point of view of social welfare, only point number (1) and (4) are reasonable for the substitution of product. It would be prudent to exclude the subsidies to equipments and privileged treatment of advertising outlays in order to make a situation when any substitution of product will upgrade consumer welfare.

Conclusion

The above discussion makes it urgent to prescribe policy for an improvement of the informal sector. According to ILO "... although the informal sector has potential for dynamic, evolutionary growth but under the existing nexus of restrictions and disincentives the seeds of involutionary growth have been sown"[(z)]. The informal sector grows up without any state support and in spite of continuous hazards. An improved policy environment will shift resources towards the informal sector allowing it to absorb the increasing labour force at higher levels of productivity (ILO '72, Weeks '73, Sethu Raman '76). Policies are then devised within an autonomy framework such as technological improvement in the informal sector (Oshima '70) or within a more integrated sector by strengthening it's link through subcontracting with the public and formal private sector by increasing the sales of informal sector products such as tools and equipments to the agricultural sector and by redistributing income in favour of the lower income groups (ILO '72, weeks '72).

The growth potential of the autonomous informal sector rests on the size of the surplus labour who are left outside the formal employment and on the possibilities of market expansion, but it suffers due to it's subordination which lies in the lack of access to resources in both input and output market. This, in turn, induces an involutionary growth. The causes of underdevelopment do not lie within the informal sector but in the process of accumulation of the central economy.

Due to the obstacles mentioned above, there would be a decrease in the share of income for the informal sector. Although it does not indicate that the informal sector will gradually disappear because the resistance factors together with market evolution will allow their survival (Souza and Tokman '76).

It can be well imagined that in the absence of any measure, there would be an involutionary growth of the informal sector due to excess supply of labour. However, evolutionary growth may also be expected but for that one should not depend only on favourable policies. To make such policies effective, they should be complemented with the variation in the distribution and allocation of surplus and with the changes in the pattern of growth. This means policies should not only be favourable to informal sector activities but also to affect directly the formal sector activities.

Whatever might be the consequence of state promotion whether progressive or merely placatory the repercussions, it is of utmost importance to the petty producers of the informal sector. There would be no improvement if the socio-economic base in which production carries on is not considered properly.

If the interest of the self-sustained and self-centered development are subservient to the domestic ruling group who themselves are the subordinates of foreign capital, how could we expect an appreciable accumulation in the informal sector?

It is rather possible that indigenous production will be stunted, distorted and exploitative than development oriented as long as the above conditions prevail.

REFERENCES

(aa) Economic and Social Survey of Asia and the Pacific, 1985 : United Nations, p. 102.

(a) Institute of social studies advisory service : "The informal sector : concepts, issues and policies" (The Hague, May '85 : Mimeographed)

(b) ILO-ARTEP, Bangladesh : Selected issues in employment and development (Bangkok, June '85) p. 1.86.

(c) Meera Mehta : "Urban informal sector : concepts, Indian evidence and policy implications" Economic and Political Weekly (Bombay, Vol. XX : no. 8, 23rd Feb. '85).

(d) S.V. Sethu Raman, ed. The urban informal sector in developing countries : Employment, poverty and environment, Geneva, ILO '81, Appendix table 4.

(e) S.V. Suthu Raman : Informal sector in Indonesia : An assessment of policies (Geneva : ILO '65).

(f) Prachom Suwatte : "Informal sector : Concept and appropriate policy, world structural change and it's impact on Asian's employment and manpower". Chira Hongladarom, ed, (Human Resource Institute : '85).

(g) Prachom Suwatte, *ibid.*, Thammasat University, Bangkok '85.

(h) please see reference 'b' above.

(i) For example, in Senegal, official sources estimate that the urban 'artisanal' population is between 30.000 and 50.000. In the Region de cap vert, the most recent figures suggest that there are 6365 urban artisanal enterprises :The urban informal sector : ed. by R. Bromley, p. 1150.

(j) In particular, the public undertakings might play a key role by providing employment in the construction of dams, roads etc. The seasonally unemployed or the unemployed in times of drought natural disasters might have a field for earning the means of living. But, the fact is, in most of the developing countries, such works have been modernized to a great extent that consequently reduces the share of public employment.

(k) Sulabha Brahme : "Producers co-operative : Experience and Lessons from India". ISS occasional papers 99. (The Hague, Institute of social studies, June '84).

(l) Victor E. Tokman : "An exploration into the nature of informal-formal sector relationship" in The urban informal sector ed. by Ray Bromley, p. 1065.

(m) Victor E. Tokman, *ibid.*, p. 1067.

(n) Oshima, H.T. : "Labour force explosion and the labour intensive sector in Asian growth", Economic development and cultural change : Vol.19, No.2, Jan.'71, p. 170.

(o) Victor E. Tokman, *ibid.*, p. 1067.

(p) Oshima ('70) does not uphold this view, since most of the persons related to this sector are, in fact, forced to dissave to survive. He solicits for such a policy in favour of the informal sector which will help to eliminate dissavings.

(q) It was found when the industrial structure of Ecuador, Peru and Venezuela were compared. The degree of structural heterogeneity found was disproportionate to the level of industrialization.See:Tokman:('74).

(r) For details, please see J. Weeks : "Policies for expanding employment in the informal urban sector of developing economies" : International Labour Review : Vol.111, No.1, January'75, p. 2.

(s) Please see Lloyd. G. Reynold : "Economic development with surplus labour : some complications" in Oxford Economic Papers (New series, London, March'69), pp. 89-103.

(t) Please see F. Stewart and J. Weeks : "The employment effects of wage changes in poor countries" discussion paper no. 8(London, department of economics, Birkbeck College, University of London, 1973)

(u) Import reproduction indicates production of the same goods domestically without using indigenous factor prices or inputs.

(v) J. Weeks : "Policies for expanding employment in the informal urban sector of developing economies" in *International Labour Review*; Vol. 111, no.1, Jan.'75, p. 10.

(w) The East African Industrial Research Organisation jointly financed by Kenya, Uganda and Tanzania, carries out such research. The ILO, for it's part, has carried out a field project in Tanzania designed to develop improved animal-drawn farming implements.

(x) J. Weeks, *ibid.*, p. 12.

(y) J. Weeks, *ibid.*, p. 12.

(z) ILO, *ibid.*, p. 505.

7

Suggestions for an Upliftment of the Garbage Pickers

The precarious existence of the garbage pickers make it necessary to suggest some way-outs which will improve their present condition. In this chapter, some of the remedies, both internal and external, have been prescribed which are, in fact, based on a field study over the related areas.

Finally, in this regard, our opinion is: the prescribed remedies could provide only a stable and better earning for the garbage pickers. But for an over-all development, we have raised some additional issues and solicited further exploration from the social scientists of future period.

Preamble

In chapter four, we have delineated the organisation of work amongst the pickers in the Bantala dumping ground that is, by nature, semi-formal. We have analysed that the garbage pickers are unlike to industrial out workers. They organise themselves at work in a special way: there is no fracas all the time amongst the pickers as one might expect from such an environment. But at the same time, the degree of trust between the pickers is too poor to work as a 'term'. Within these features, the garbage pickers of Bantala organise themselves at work.

Although, in the micro level, there is the existence of perennial poverty, but in the macro level, there is a good indication of entrepreneurship and innovative capacity. The garbage pickers of Bantala consider the petty buyers as the pillar of success and believe that there is a little more money to earn in the dumping ground. But a countable number of pickers are not motivated towards this 'belief'. Perhaps, this is the reason why they do like only to defend their right to work and cannot go ahead, irrespective of the prevailing barriers, by making enough money.

What we have analysed in the previous chapter can be summed up as follows: the activities in the garbage dump constitute work that generates income for the pickers and provides a supply of essential inputs for the industrial economy. The garbage pickers are not unskilled, unproductive, unorganized or unenterprising. But the manner in which they are carrying out their daily operation is neither one that could improve their pecuniary condition in the long run, nor it could uproot the barriers that prevail in the mid way.

Indeed, we should think of policies that will make this picking activity a stable one and at the same time will enhance the level of income of the pickers. Considering these aspects, we suggest here the following remedies:

PART ONE

External Remedies

(A) The Bio-Gas Plant

The CMC is going to start a pilot project for generating BIOGAS from municipal solid waste in collaboration with Burn Standard Company. According to the official source[a], this project will start it's operation within the middle of 1989. The location selected for this project is adjacent to the Bantala check post where the preliminary work like installation of essential machineries has already been completed.

This project will generate biogas from organic vegetable matter like vegetable waste, banana leaves etc. In order to obtain the basic raw material, the CMC has a plan for utilizing the market garbage of Calcutta[b]. The daily requirement or such raw material will amount to 500 Kgs.

The basic object of this project is to utilise garbage in different purpose. The authorities consider this project most urgent because along with other benefits, it will control air pollution by reducing the quantity of market garbage. The biogas plant, as reported by the officials of the CMC, will serve three sectors. These are household sector, industrial sector and agricultural sector. In the former sector, biogas can be utilised for lighting up the domestic oven while in the industrial sector, it can be used for running the generator. In the latter sector, the disposed slurry of this plant can be utilised for soil conditioning.

The required land for implementing this project has already been provided by the CMC, which will be responsible for maintenance, production and supervision. The Burn Standard Company will provide necessary finance in this project. At present, this project is in its final stage. The CMERI of Durgapur has framed the design of this project. (Please see note 'a') which shares the responsibility of installation and trial of the machineries. Both the CMC and the CMERI are the autonomous body while the Burn Standard Company is a Govt. of India Undertaking. The department of non-conventional energy system, Govt. of India, is the central authority of this project.

The processes related to the production of bio-gas has been planned by the CMC in the following manner:

In the first process, market garbage will be stored in the platform inside the workshop by the municipal trucks. Initially, three trucks of such waste material will be needed. The market garbage will be disposed of from municipal truck through tipping gear. This is a totally mechanized process.

In process two the required material will be sorted out manually. In particular, organic vegetable matter will be separated manually from a variety of waste material usually found in the city garbage [c]. According to the official source, this process cannot be converted into a mechanical one.

In the third process, the material, so sorted out, will be washed clearly with the help of trommel (a mechanical device). There will be manual charging for putting the material inside the trammel. The latter will be operated by one semi-skilled personnel preferably having some knowledge in electricity and maintenance. The manual work involved in this process (i.e. charging material inside the trommel) may be carried out by any unskilled worker. The authority is looking for such personnel for this job who are within twenty-five years of age. This process is, therefore, partly mechanical and partly manual.

In the fourth process, there will be size reduction of the organic vegetable matter in order to bring them to the desired size. Two machines, namely, Shredder and Chaffe-Cutter, will perform this work. In order to operate these machines, there will be the need of skilled machine men. In addition, there will be manual feeding to both the machines. This latter work does not require any skill; hence, it is open for unskilled worker.

Process five involves the charging of raw material (i.e. the organic vegetable matter) inside the digestor manually. This particular process of work is virtually open to anybody since the job does not require any specialization. The authority, however, likes to carry out this function mechanically with the expansion of the project.

There after, biogas will be generated inside the digestor automatically. There would be a time gap of fourteen days between the first charging of raw materials inside the digestor and the first production of biogas. As daily charging will continue, the biogas so generated, will be collected in a gasholder. Finally, it will produce electricity through the operation of generator. The latter requires a skilled operator who will switch it on and will be responsible for its maintenance. The authority likes to appoint a person with ITI (electrical) diploma preferably having three/four years experience in similar job.

There is ample opportunity for the garbage pickers to grow up with this project, as a number of processes included therein require a very simple manual operation. These are, specifically, process number two in full and process number three, four and five in part. Though, process number five may be converted into a mechanical one in future, but at present, this can well be considered as a manual process.

Therefore, we may consider this project as a potential source of alternative employment for the garbage pickers. The latter with their present level of skill and productivity may easily be absorbed in the processes mentioned above. The officials have a positive view towards the garbage pickers. They agree with us that the latter with their in born experience might have a good role to play in this project. The policy makers, while planning for the personnel required for this project, should consider this particular section of labour with due importance. We have already mentioned that this is a pilot project. What we are yet to mention is that as a source of non-conventional energy, the biogas has an increasing demand in the present market, one might presume a bright future of this project. To counsel for an articulation of the garbage pickers with this project is justified in all respect. Specially, if we consider that this project will not only improve their earnings but also exploit their productivity and skill in a proper perspective.

(B) The Compost Plant[(d)]

The West Bengal Agro Industries Corporation Limited has started to produce manure near Bantala dumping ground since 1976. The types of raw materials required for producing manure are domestic garbage, night soil and refuse of beasts. The daily requirement of raw material is between 125 to 150 metric tones while the output is on an average 70 metric tones. Such manure is generally used in order to make the land more fertile and has a long-term effect. Because, although it may not initially boost up the production of crops which can be done by using chemical manure, but in comparison with the latter, the manure produced by the West Bengal Agro Industries, is more beneficial in the sense that the chemical manure affects the fertility of land by making the soil porous in the long run while this adversity can be checked by utilizing this manure.

This project is under the control of the state Govt. of West Bengal. The top management consists of one chairman;

one managing director and one general manager, under the latter there are four executive engineers. Twenty-seven personnel of whom the majority possesses technical qualifications carry out the daily production.

The process of work starts with the disposing of garbage by the tipping gear from municipal trucks that are put to the apron feeder with the help of pay loader. Thus, the initial process is a complete mechanical process.

In the second process all unwanted materials like stones, glass pieces, leather etc. are eliminated from garbage. This process, therefore, involves in sorting of the garbage that is carried out manually.

In the third process, the materials, so sorted, are sent to the pulveriser from apron feeder through conveyer belt that crushes the materials in order to make it powdery. Like the initial process, the work of this process is also operated by mechanical device completely.

In the forth process, the materials, so crushed, are sent to drum mixture through conveyer belt which, in turn, sends the same to window yard through discharge conveyer. This is also a mechanical process.

In the fifth process, the dust of garbage is kept in the window yard for maturing through natural process, specifically, through sunshine. In this process, very simple manual operation is needed for dressing and redressing of the dust of garbage in the sunlight so as to dry it up quickly.

In the sixth process, the matured dust of garbage is taken to screening yard manually. Any person, capable of carrying weight, may perform this job. After screening, the residues are removed manually while the fine dusts are packing also manually. However, the authority has a plan to carry out this function mechanically in future.

The disclosure of the process of work involved in the manufacturing of manure clearly indicates that there are processes that need very simple manual operation. These are process number two, five and six. But, before going to enmark them a potential for alternative employment for the garbage pickers, we should consider some of the basic facts that are narrated below:

Firstly, so long the authority does not employ any outsiders for carrying out that simple manual operation, as discussed above, other than their own labour force. The authority, at the time of this interview, did not make any positive sign so that it could be anticipated that the garbage pickers may be absorbed in future period. According to the officials, their own labour force is sufficient to carry out the necessary functions, be it mechanical or manual, even in far future.

Secondly, the project itself is not operating for more than two years. As a result, the authority has withdrawn the workers and the employees concerned with this project. They are, however, absorbed in different venture under the same authority. The reasons for such haulting of work have not been explained by the authority that only discloses that there were some 'internal reasons' behind such cease work. The authority describes such 'internal reasons' as 'confidential'. We have been informed that the project will be in operation very soon.

Lastly, there is no plan to modify or expand this project. An attempt of the concerned authority is at present confined to re-open the plant only.

The above analysis makes it clear that this manure plant may not act as a potential source for alternative employment for the garbage pickers. Though the project has several processes which are suitable for the latter, but taking into account the present condition of the project, non-existence of any plan for future modification or expansion and, in addition, the policy like employment of own labour force, make this project beyond reach for the garbage pickers.

Besides, the CMC had two more proposals for setting one compactor plant and one incinerator plant. Unfortunately, these proposals had not been materialized due to the high requirement of capital for their necessary implementation. In these plants also, there were job opportunity for the garbage pickers. One point is clear from the discussion we held with the executive engineers of the CMC : whatever might be the method for utilizing garbage for different purposes, it always relates to a common process, namely, sorting of garbage, which can never be performed mechanically. For this particular operation, the CMC would have to depend always on such labourers as the garbage pickers.

Conclusion

It would be prudent, therefore, to suggest that the more is the growth of different plants for multipurpose use of garbage, the more is the potential for alternative employment for the garbage pickers. Of course, this is not by any means to suggest that only for the sake of employment of the garbage pickers, such plants should be built up. In true sense, the garbage pickers have an in-depth knowledge about the vivid kinds of waste materials that are available in the dumping ground along with their exact location and approximate quantity so available. If this 'knowledge' can be tapped properly, it might innovate new methods for utilizing garbage more suitably. In one occasion, a scientist of CMERI had been informed by a garbage picker about the plentiful availability of JHILLI (one type of garbage), which is the most desirable component for producing methane gas. The scientist, himself, confessed to us that he was totally ignorant about the existence of JHILLI in Bantala dumping ground and if he is asked to propose for a new plant by the top authority of the CMERI in future, he will submit a scheme for generating methane gas in Bantala.

And we would like to stress on this point. There should be an exchange of opinion between the authority and the garbage pickers before starting up any new project. The former will get the 'cream' of knowledge that the latter possess traditionally. This might, in turn, have an effect to make the project more stable and profitable. And the latter will get the benefit of employment from the setting up of such new project. Hence, there would be mutual benefit that will bring grist to both mills.

PART TWO

Internal Remedy

One of the ways out of improving the monetary condition of the garbage picker is to form a co-operative amongst them. The bulk quantities of materials sold regularly by the garbage pickers can be made more profitable if the individual sale is converted into a sale through co-operative. The pickers might receive two-fold benefits: Firstly, they will get comparatively better price whenever they will sale to the co-operative, because the co-operative, itself, will get a better price, through bargaining. The latter will be possible because the co-operative will hold a lump-sum quantity of materials. Secondly, the surplus earned by the co-operative may be distributed to the garbage pickers. The nature of the waste materials collected by the pickers is not perishable. If a certain quantity of these materials can be hoard from the daily collection, it might pay

TABLE 1.23

The Seasonal Fluctuation in the Price of Waste Material

Average Price

Season	*Paper*	*Iron*	*Glass*	*Plastic*		*Aluminium*
				Soft	*hard*	
	Per (Kg In Rs.)	*Per (Kg In Rs.)*	*Per (Kg In Rs.)*	*Per (Kg*	*In Rs.)*	*Per (Kg In Rs.)*
Summer	.45	2.50	.35	14.00	12.00	20.00
Autumn	.60	3.70	.55	18.50	17.25	32.50
Winter	.50	1.60	.30	12.00	11.00	23.25

more dividends to the co-operative. This is because of the fact that there is seasonal fluctuation in the price of waste materials. The date, we collect from field survey, will enumerate this point properly. This is furnished in the table 1.23 :

It is evident from above that the price of waste materials increases in autumn. In winter, such prices come down comparatively than summer (other than paper and aluminum). As all of the above mentioned materials are storable for some time, the co-operative might enhance its surplus by selling largely in autumn.

The above also presents a picture of 'normal' price fluctuation of waste material in different seasons. Besides, according to the garbage pickers, there are occasional boosting up of prices of certain material which encourage the pickers to collect that particular material in bulk quantities. Consequently, the price comes down and the pickers suffer loss. Such loss can be checked if the co-operative has its own warehouse to store waste materials. The 'warehouse' could provide a good contribution in the earning of the garbage pickers at the time of both normal and occasional fluctuation of prices of waste materials.

However, to form a co-operative amongst the garbage pickers is not so simple as it sounds. Firstly, the garbage pickers, themselves do not believe in 'team' work. As we have seen already, the total activities related to garbage picking is highly self-depending. The garbage pickers do rely on individual capacity. This cannot be changed overnight, nor can we expect something like that. There should be proper campaigning, highlighting specifically, the benefits of a co-operative, amongst the garbage pickers. This may not be fruitful in the short run but, in the long run, there might be a change in the outlook of the garbage pickers.

Secondly, it is difficult to find out a suitable location for establishing warehouse whereby materials will be preserved for selling at a future period. Neither it is possible to set up in the area where the pickers reside because of its narrow space and congestion, nor it is possible to set up within the dumping ground as the Municipal Act forbids it. (Off the track, it can also be noted that according to this Act., garbage picking within the dumping ground itself is illegal).

Eyeing the above difficulties, it is doubtful whether any co-operative will at all be formed amongst the garbage pickers even in far future. Therefore, we could suggest that initially such an effort should come from outside, specially, from some social organisation with a keen desire for improving the pecuniary condition of these marginalised masses. This might have an impressive effect on the garbage pickers than mere campaign in favour of co-operative society. There is every possibility that once a co-operative is formed and the pickers witness its benefit, they will react accordingly. However, it can be well imagined that such a co-operative would have to face a cut throat competition with the 'standard' buyers of Tangra.

Summing Up

The above remedies will induce stability in the primary stratum of the recuperative work and an incremental effect on the present level of income of the garbage pickers. Yet, these are the recommendations for the present period only. In the long run, question may arise as to how far it is viable to plan for financial improvement alone? Especially when, there is clear indication of entrepreneurship and innovative capacity amongst the garbage pickers whatever little it may be, we should not forget that these marginalized masses are so characterized in such an environment that is wantonly severe. If it is the fact why don't we provide them an environment where such inherent features could evolve properly which might be helpful for the rest of the society?

And here lies the main issue. What would be our future outlook towards these labourers? Should we discharge our liability by providing only some alternative sources of earning for them? Or, should we proceed in a planned way for utilizing the latent potential of the garbage pickers for an overall development of our society? Is it possible at all in the prevailing social set up?

These are some of the interrogatives on which further exploration is most welcome from the social scientists of future period.

REFERENCES

(a) This portion of our study is based on the information provided by the executive engineers of the CMC and the scientists of the CMERI (Central Mechanical Engineering Research Institute) of Durgapur. We held an interview with these top-ranking personnel in February '89.

(b) Initially, the garbage of Baitakkhana market, Gariahat market and Barabazar Fal Patty (Fruit Centre) will be utilised.

(c) It is interesting to note here the physical analysis of Calcutta refuge which is as follows: Leaves: 13.052%; Garbage: 16.053%; Hay & Straw : 6.312%; Coconut shell pieces : 4.959%; Paper : 3.178%; Rags : 3.602%; Ash & Earth : 33.585%; Ignited Coal : 8.083%; Earthen Ware : 6.649; Stone : 1.833%; Iron & Metal: .6624%; Bones: .4200%; Leáther : .8624%; Polythene & Plastic : .6456%; Glass : .3795%. This analysis is the average of a number of samples collected in this regard: Source: Feasibility studies for Calcutta city: a report of the Central Public Health Engineering Research Institute: Nagpur : 3.

(d) We are indebted to the top management of the respective authority for providing us with the relevant information in this regard. We held this interview in March '89.

8

Strategies for an All Round Development of the Informal Sector

In this chapter we disclose some strategies for an overall development of the informal sector. For this purpose we have highlighted the report of a seminar concerning informal sector held in Kenya '72. In our opinion, this will help to prescribe policies in a broad perspective even today.

Our concluding remark is that as the informal sector by itself, is a new phenomenon, first of all a broad contour of it should be framed properly which will spell out every aspect of the informal sector. This, in turn, will let a space for prescribing education and training system as well as technology that are 'appropriate' and 'applicable' to this sector. The employment potential of this informal sector can be utilised only when this 'basic' work is completed.

PREAMBLE

In the developing countries there grow a consciousness about the failure of the economic growth. Most of the government of such countries is aware about how to increase the productive employment and how to upgrade the earning of the poorest section of the populace. In these countries, unemployment, under employment and extreme poverty started mounting since late '60's.

At the same time, there is a positive sign in the planning and policies of these developing countries towards a new development strategy that will have an impact on the level of employment. Such strategies will also multiple the benefit of growth in a way so that the downtrodden might have a right share of it.

In response to the framing out of such a broad strategy, the ILO world employment programme committee held two seminars[(a)] — one relates to study and the other is on policy making — simultaneously at Limuru in Kenya in '72.

The study seminar examined the different elements of a comprehensive employment strategy and considered it's effect on planning procedure while the objects of the policy seminar were, in the one hand, to let an opportunity for the policy makers to exchange opinions on selected key issues of employment strategy and, on the other hand, to utilise the 'cream' of such opinions in the topics they had been examining. The whole discussion of the policy seminar was limited to some fundamentals to an employment strategy which were, firstly, employment in the small scale and informal sector; secondly, appropriate technology in an employment strategy; thirdly, wages and incomes policy as a component of employment strategy and fourthly, education and training policies as they relate to employment problems.

The primary functions of the policy seminar were two fold: (1) to examine the limit of applicability of the ideas and policy prescriptions presented in the Kenya mission report[(b)]; (2) to send pilot employment mission to different countries for (a) prescribing specific suggestions to the respective governments and (b) spreading a demonstration effect on other countries in the same region.

Considering the prevailing economic conditions, the

Kenya employment report[c] suggests for a speedy promotion of the informal sector and defines it as consists of variety of activities (e.g. small traders, manufacturers etc.) where production process is highly labour intensive. The lower income group mainly creates the demand for the final output of this sector. According to this report, it is not altogether true that this sector provides job opportunity only to the casual or unproductive workers. The Kenya Government considered the report "refreshingly innovative on the subject of the informal sector and generally accepts its recommendations".

The report also illustrates clearly that for the purpose of generating more employment, there would be the need of changing technology. The latter involves in expanding a narrow circle by way of altering income distribution, by altering relative price of workers and by improving and implementing machine-tools, products and techniques in a way most suitable with the altered income distribution and relative price of workers. The Government of Kenya declared that it is "sympathetic with the objective of changing the mix of products produced in favour of those which are labour intensive and which are consumed by low-income groups".

On the question of wages and incomes policy, the Kenya report held a view that in order to be effective, such a policy should be considered as an impartial segment of the employment approach to development and not simply as a rectifying method for adverse social consequences of a development plan which is basically need-oriented. The Government of Kenya agreed, "The time has come to formulate more specific guidelines for the development of wages and other incomes".

Finally, in the matter of education and training, the Kenya report found that the problem of school leavers could be solved by proper distribution of income, specifically, by abolishing the imbalance between aspirations and employment opportunities. Based on the choice of the Kenya people as well as on the types of prevailing and potential employment opportunities, the report prescribed a job linked educational system. The Kenyan Government accepted it because "(it) would leave the country with an educational system in the next decade which is radically different from the system which it now possesses."

Focusing on Some Aspects of Informal Sector

The discussion held in the seminar concerning the informal sector was centered round the discontinuities of the features of this sector. A good many of the seminar participants pointed out the wide disparities in the level of income, size of the units and technology between this sector and the rest of the economy. They considered such discontinuities as a consequence of features inherent in small-scale enterprises.

In the seminar, several arguments were raised by the participants that can be summarized as follows:

The technology of the west though may not be ideal but superior to developing countries. It can be adopted by the large enterprises but it is not accessible to the small entrepreneurs. There is no competition between these two segments of the economy either in respect of resources or for customer. Hence, any policy favours the growth of formal sector, does not in any respect hinders that of informal sector. Even if, it is harmful for the latter, that is due to the inevitable consequence of the struggle between superior and inferior. The upholder of this view conceded that although the fostering of industrial technology "across the board" might have some negative impact on the level of employment but it can be solved without any encouragement of the informal sector which is mostly either inefficient or survive without any growth potential. However, according to this view, there should not be any restrictions for the informal sector.

The another argument which might be called 'structural disadvantages' was just the reverse; it ran as follows:

> The large-scale industries are superior because of the state support by way of implementing favourable policies. Otherwise, there is every doubt how far they could compete with the small enterprises, if the privileges enjoyed by them are also offered to the latter. In fact, the latter is inefficient due to the consequence of the structure of an economy where policy prescriptions protect the former. The so-called 'superior' technology of the large-scale industries is not so much of 'higher' quality as of 'irrelevant' quality. While, there is, in fact, the need of 'improved' products which can easily be made by indigenous materials and indigenous skills.

Thus, there is a clear-cut delimitation. According to the former argument the informal sector is characterized by some 'inherent backwardness' while according to the latter argument such backwardness is created due to 'structural' disadvantage. The former does not agree that the 'discontinuities' in an economy are due to the adsorption of privileges by the large-scale industries while the latter rejects the fact that the technology of the large enterprises is inherently superior.

The seminar also provides broad views about two topics: namely, whether the informal sector is transitory or permanent? And, whether there is a complementary or competing relationship between the formal and the informal sector?

The implication of the former view seems to be that how long the informal sector survives as such rests on how fast employment generates in this sector. The latter view, on the other hand, expresses that the 'gap' between formal and informal sector can be reduced provided proper and wider distribution of resources is made. Of course, in such a situation, both these sectors will be temporary because of their merger into a single sector.

However, the participants of the seminar were agreed to one point: There are some specific activities carried on in the informal sector which have no future potential i.e. nothing can be done to raise the earnings of those who are related to these activities.

On the other hand, there was no unity of opinion as to whether the economic activities of the informal sector which have a growth potential in future should be encouraged or not. Nevertheless, an agreement was made on the ground that there should not be any 'rigid' policies applicable to the informal sector of all developing countries. To be effective, such a policy must be flexible enough. For example, policies applicable to a developing country where informal trading, manufacturing activities etc. are traditional may not be fruitful for a developing country where such activities are developed more recently.

There was also diversity of opinion on the question what should be the outlook of the government towards this sector? According to the opinion of some of the participants who considered this sector as inefficient, the government should provide 'minimum' support towards this sector while others thought that 'maximum' support is must for exploiting the productivity of this sector. Due to this disagreement, formulation of specific policies on credit, diffusion of information etc., were not feasible.

Selection of an Appropriate Technology: Some Relevant Steps

The seminar's view about the suitable technology of a developing country can be categorized as (i) conceptual framework of an 'appropriate' technology (ii) the identification of appropriate techniques and (iii) the introduction and implementation of these techniques.

Defining the term 'appropriate' technology in the context of a developing country, the seminar held such a view that a technology is appropriate only when it is job-oriented and can raise the incomes of the working poor who, in spite of long working hours, earn a little and still in the poverty level. Besides, it should use minimum amount of capital and should let a wide scope for utilizing the plentiful manpower. In addition, it should be flexible enough so that it can be adjusted to the local environment either socially or institutionally.

However, it was noted that such a technology mostly is associated with the small-scale enterprises of the informal sector. Such enterprises are highly labour intensive as well as advantageous in the sense that the employment of family labour makes wages non-existing or very negligible.

After reviewing the ways of improving appropriate technologies, the following methods had been spelled out.

Firstly: to raise the prevailing levels of technology of the informal sector in a gradual manner and thus to upgrade the productivity and earnings of the working masses.

Secondly: to adopt the imported technology and make a proper use of it by way of adjusting the same with the existing local conditions. Such adjustment includes redesigning of indigenous equipment and utilizing imported machineries for more hours per day (as it was done in Japan).

Thirdly: to innovate new labour intensive techniques by allocating resources for research and development, which will help to discover the new production methods alongwith, their commercial application.

As in practice, the choice of technology is very limited, it was emphasized that an object like creation of employment can be fulfilled by shifting technology not only towards labour intensity but also towards the production of such products that are consumed by mass people. The market for labour intensive products can be enlarged provided the income is redistributed in favour of the poorer classes. But as such products are of poor quality, it was decided that proper steps should be taken for quality control and product diversification.

For the purpose of identifying appropriate technologies, it was considered that both their direct and indirect employment effects should be counted. The following are the examples which might be viewed as appropriate technology[(d)]

- In agriculture, small instead of large tractors, animal drawn instead of hand ploughs and multiple cropping instead of single cropping.
- In manufacturing, semi-automatic instead of automatic processes, power-driven grating machines for manufacturing block-making and mixing machines.
- in construction, agricultural tractors to pull trailers, rollers etc.
- in services, small scale retailers instead of chain stores and super markets.

Due to the communication gap between the developed and the developing countries or between the formal and the informal sector of the developing countries, the existing appropriate technology that could provide mass employment opportunity, does not find the media for a wide circulation. Besides, sometimes labour intensive technologies are impeded by the lack of adequate management or supervisory skills. For example, in construction work, there is the employment of numerous unskilled workers that at the same time requires an adequate number of supervisors.

However, in order to utilise the imported technology, which is, in fact, based on the needs of the developed countries, the developing countries should gear up their national technological capacity and know-how. Moreover, there should be a selective approach to the imported technology[e].

In order to introduce and implement appropriate technologies, the policy measures should be classified as: price and other incentives; appropriate management, planning and organisation and other means of action. The discussion of the seminar under these groups is summarized below[f].

Price and Other Incentives

1. Lower interest rates on loans for second-hand imported machinery and locally produced equipment.
2. Tax rebates on training costs incurred by multinational firms or large scale local firms in providing apprentice training schemes and management development programmes.
3. Financial transfers from the government to the private sector (in the form of wage subsidies, for example) for specific activities or projects (e.g. road construction). This is necessary where switching over to a labour-intensive technology increases a private entrepreneur's financial costs.
4. Selective taxes on imports of certain types of equipment for which local substitutes are available; customs duties and indirect (sales) taxes on luxury products in order to encourage the production and consumption of local products.

Appropriate Management, Planning and Organisation

1. Decentralized management and supervision to ensure effective use of labour-intensive methods in construction; Delegation of authority and responsibility at work sites is likely to lead to higher labour productivity and speedier completion of work.

2. Use of 'labour only' contracts specifying a minimum amount of labour to be used in road construction.
3. To import modern technology and export labour intensive products through negotiation with the multinational companies.

Other Means of Action

1. To establish technological information centres with a view to improve communication system. Such centres should provide information relating to technical specifications of existing machines, tools etc., labour requirement (both skilled and unskilled), input requirement, repair and maintenance costs etc.
2. Channelling of available research and development resources to the real needs. Enmarking of a greater proportion of such resources as the needs of the informal sector.
3. Reorientation of the work of research and development centres to meet the requirements of smaller enterprises in the informal sector.

Policy of Distributing Wages and Incomes

In the developing countries, the underlying socio-economic structure determines the pattern of wealth and income distribution. Such pattern is changed either i) by the political and economic power or ii) by the pressure of the market.

In fact, the improper distribution of wealth and income is highly related to the employment problem. Firstly, if the latter problem involves both creation of job opportunities and raising of the level of incomes of the working poor, an unequal distribution of income automatically intensifies this problem. Secondly, there is an indirect effect of income distribution on the growth of employment opportunities through savings and capital accumulation; unequal distribution of income affects such growth.

The income structure also has far reaching impact on different aspects of development policy. Firstly, it affects the types of product manufactured in a country as well as the technology used. Secondly, it affects the size and growth of the informal sector. Thirdly, it determines, to some extent, the level of rural-urban migration and thus of urban unemployment. It is clear, therefore, an income policy should be integrated into an overall development strategy.

Reviewing the prevailing structure and trends of income distribution, it appears that in most of the developing countries, there exist such structures and trends of income as are partly inherited from colonial past and partly pursued by the policies implemented since independence.

The inequalities as evident in the developing countries in this regard are of two types: Firstly, there is a minority class consisting of large landlords, renters, professionals, big businessmen and highly skilled personnel. They are enormously affluent than the masses. Secondly, the semi-skilled or unskilled workers of the modern sector have been able to upgrade the income levels through organized movement. Their income is lower than the affluent minority class but higher than the peasants and the working masses of the informal sector.

However, these inequalities are rather increasing over the past decade due to i) the transfer of high incomes and assets to a small number of indigenous people and ii) the regressive distribution of benefits deriving from government expenditure.

The objectives of the wages and incomes policy of a developing country may be outlined as under: i) to promote rapid employment and earning opportunity, ii) to promote more egalitarian distribution of wealth and income, iii) to allocate resources efficiently and to provide more incentives for greater mobility of factors of production.

Of course, the importance of the above objectives may not be equal always. For a country, where economic equality exists already, there should be a greater emphasis on the incentives objective. While for a country with lack of income equality, greater priority should be allowed to the objective of egalitarianism.

A comprehensive policy must concern itself not only with all types of income – wages, salaries, profits, dividends, rents etc., but also with all sectors of the economy – agriculture, mining, manufacturing and services. It should take into account the objectives of income policy. More specifically, government expenditure and taxation, foreign exchange rate policy, patterns of investment etc. should re-inforce the central thrusts of an income policy.

However, in order to be successful, an income policy must provide room for sufficient redistribution of assets. The suggestable guidelines might include land reform and public participation in enterprises and sectors of strategic importance to the economy like banks, insurance companies, housing supply of products of mass consumption etc.

If, for any reasons, redistribution policies like public ownership or land reform are not possible or desirable, direct controls might be enforced on prices, rents, dividends etc. This might create black markets in the products or services where such control is imposed. To avoid it, indirect measures might be more effective which include import liberalization to control both the prices and profits of local enterprises, the raising of bank rates, public provision of mass consumption goods and services, so as to keep their prices low by increasing their supply.

It is, however, difficult to reduce the income gap among the personnel of different sectors. Though, it does not create serious problem while imposing a policy of wage freeze in the public sector but in the private sector, it is not effective as it encourages only under the table payment.

Due to this difficulty, it is necessary to trace out the conditions on which the success of a policy of wage restraint depends. These include i) to control inflation and to make the cost of living of workers stable, ii) to ensure that the prices of products and services benefiting from productivity increases are reduced and iii) to assure that increased profits are siphoned off for additional investment and creation of more employment.

Of course, the realities of the power structure of the developing countries are such that there is a little scope of applying technical solution to the problem of poverty and unequal distribution of wealth and income. The participants of the seminar, therefore, considered that a fundamental change in the power structure of the society to be a prerequisite for an egalitarian development strategy.

Education and Training in Relation to Employment

The complete discussion of the seminar relating to above can be described under the following points,— two of it is preliminary and others are matter of policy.

Point 1: It highlights the nature of employment problem and it's relation with educated unemployment. The employment problem, as discussed in the seminar, covers both the open unemployment and the problem of working poor. In most of the developing countries, the latter is no less important than the former. Another aspect highlighted in this regard is the underutilization of available human resources.

The educated unemployment had been defined as the mismatch between the aspirations of school leavers on the one hand and the available job opportunities on the other. Therefore, it is not the major cause that there is lack of job opportunity rather the major cause is job opportunities do not correspond to the expectation of the school leavers. This is the consequence of the fact that school system has not been able to cope with the prevailing needs of trade and commercial sectors.

Point 2: The education and training system has a good role to play in the employment problem, particularly in the educated unemployment problem. Besides education and training system, various economic and social factors should also be considered in this regard as these are equally responsible for this problem. Therefore, if there is a change in the education and training system so as to minimize unemployment, proper care should be taken to the factors outside the education and training syllabus which should also be rectified in order to make new education and training policies more effective. Moreover, it was held in the seminar that school certificates and academic degrees should not be the only determinants of the kind of job people get or of their promotion in future. Though, it is beyond argument that more job opportunities must be created in the informal sector and in the rural areas but before creating such possibilities, it would not be wise, according to the opinion of the participants of the seminar, to stress on informal types of education and training.

Point 3: There is the need to identify the structural and qualitative change which must be made in the education and training system in relation to the unemployment problem. It was decided in the seminar, that more emphasis should be given on innovative and problem-solving skills in the school curricula and the present system of learning by rote and memorizing facts and figures should be avoided. This will help the majority of school leavers who would have to create their own job by becoming self-employed. Besides, changes in the content of education, it was proposed that examination system should also be rectified. There should be the introduction of such tests, which focus on problem-solving skills and intellectual versatility. Such changes in the examination system should be widely publicized in order to provide necessary opportunity to the teaching staff to adopt this new system.

Point 4: The above necessitates an introduction of comprehensive teacher retraining programme. Once the matters included in point 3 are changed, there would be no problem to introduce a retraining programme.

Point 5: There should be redistribution of resources in favour of basic education. As in most of the developing countries, more resources are allocated to secondary and higher education, the participants of the seminar considered that this situation should no longer be continued.

Point 6: Highlighting the need that post basic education should be closely related to the requirements of the society, it was agreed in the seminar that there should be the implementation of recurrent education system. This system of education i) combines both formal and informal education and training system in a consistent whole and ii) spreads the educational system in such a way so that people could easily move in and out according to their motivation and changing employment opportunities. The recurrent education system will make post basic education more flexible. It could easily be adjusted according to the changes in the labour market.

Point 7: One striking fact, specially, about the workers of the informal sector is that a majority of them either never go to school or are early drop outs. To tackle this problem, it was proposed in the seminar that imaginative informal training centres must be set up so that such people might have a second chance to cope with the trend of education and training system.

Conclusion

The great merit of the seminar was that it placed the employment objective at the centre of planning. To upgrade the level of employment, several aspects had been scrutinised in the seminar. A developing country must consider such a technology, that will utilise its manpower excessively and hence, should be labour intensive.

On the question of education and training, the seminar recommended some fundamental changes if it is to generate new employment opportunity.

However, one might consider the discussion of the seminar on the informal sector merely conceptual. As this sector is one of the recent phenomenons of the developing country's economy, it will take some extra time for an intellectual framework applicable to this sector.

REFERENCES

(a) The institute for development studies of the University of Nairobi and the institute of development studies of the University of Sussex organized these seminars jointly.

(b) For a full length view, please see ILO : Employment, Incomes and Equality : A strategy for increasing productive employment in Kenya (Geneva, 1972).

(c) As described in the session paper on employment (No. 10 of 1973).

(d) "A new look at some strategies for increasing productive employment in Africa" : Louis Emmerij : International Labour Review : Vol. 110; No. 3, Sept. '74, p. 207.

(e) See K. Marsden : "Progressive technologies for developing countries" : International Labour Review, May'70, p. 475-502.

(f) For details, please see Louis Emmerij, *ibid.*, pp. 207-209.

9

Informal Sector in the Indian Context

The most urgent task of an underdeveloped economy is to eradicate unemployment and poverty. This, in turn, requires such a sector where mass employment is possible. In this study, we have identified and analysed the determinants of employment in the informal sector. In our opinion, this sector can act as a mass labour absorber. In this chapter, we exhibit some valuable comments on unemployment with context to India where primary sector like agriculture has a little role to play on this problem. It is justified to make a complementary relation between formal and informal sector and thus to avoid technological unemployment which is a noted root of unemployment in most of the developing country including India. Thereafter, some aspects of investment in a developing country have been described with a view to see whether it is justified to invest in the informal sector. However, it is realized that there is every justification to solicit fresh investment for this sector.

As we realize the importance of the informal sector with context to India, we then formulate suggestive schemes for an overall development of the informal sector. These suggestive schemes will be more effective, if it is based on definite programmes. For this reason, we have mentioned some programmes, which might assist the scheme to a great extent. In the conclusion, we have raised two crucial questions that should be considered before going to implement any development project for the informal sector.

Preamble

In an economy where under employment and unemployment is most predominant, high rates of labour absorption indicates a redistribution of income. Under such conditions, the formulation of a comprehensive employment policy is the first step towards alleviating unemployment and poverty. Experience demonstrates that modern industrial sectors, because of a high propensity to import capital-intensive technologies, are less sensitive to labour. So, policies designed to raise employment must be supported by diversified strategies: But what is more needed is to search for new employment opportunities in the existing productive structure.

The unplanned sector, commonly known as the informal sector, of developing country's economy is such a sector where mass employment opportunity exists. We have already proved the employment potential of this particular sector. India, being a developing country, suffers largely from unemployment problem. Informal sector can play a good role in this regard. For a better understanding, we would like to present here a summarized view of our study, which highlights several aspects of the informal sector.

Indian Context

So far as India's case is considered, it would be prudent to solicit for a policy, which will maximize the level of employment with minimum cost. As evident from above discussion, informal sector could satisfy both these criteria. In a different way, Schumacher pointed out "The problem of unemployment in poor section is solvable only if one achieves… industrial structure which enable the people …… to use their labour power for providing most of their basic requirements themselves"[(a)]. Such an industrial structure can be framed within the informal sector in a sense that in the informal sector, the basic requirements of the marginalized masses are produced by themselves.

In India, the unemployment problem becomes acute from the post independence era, which could not be minimized even by introducing the programme of five years planning. It is better to accept the basic fact that the relevant strategies for solving unemployment have well sunk.

In view of the emerging problem of unemployment which is politically and socially undesirable, the Bhagavati Committee observed "... If additional employment opportunities are created in the secondary and tertiary sectors some workers should invariably be withdrawn from the primary sector to the secondary or tertiary sectors to lighten the burden of the former sector"[(b)].

According to a recent survey[(c)], the agricultural sector in India could provide a little scope for additional employment. In fact, if the excess burden of manpower is withdrawn from agriculture, the net output per worker would be much higher. Besides, in rural India, the problem of unemployment is realized severely among the landless labourers.

The unemployment problem of India can be solved to some extent, if proper attention is paid for utilizing the employment potential of the informal sector (the employability of this sector has already been shown in tabular form in chapter six). It is also noteworthy that such a voluminous employment is provided with no or very little official assistance. To stress on this sector might solve two purposes: firstly, mass employment will be possible and secondly, there would be a diffusing effect to strengthen the base of the overall economy.[(d)]

J. Tinbergen openly solicited in favour of an efficient

and competitive labour intensive production system (which is a chief feature of the informal sector activities). In his opinion ".... To all countries, to their planners, to their industrialists that whenever labour intensive activities are efficient whenever they are competitive in the world market such activities should be maintained and expanded."[e] The ILO also shares this opinion from different point of view: " .... The employment targets incorporated in development plans of many developing countries are quite low. Often targets are just sufficient to absorb the additions to the labour force but not high enough to reduce substantially the existing unemployment.. It is necessary, therefore, to explore the possibility of using more labour intensive technique".[f]

As most of the developing countries are characterized by plethora of labour and scarcity of capital, the planners should utilise the employment potential of the informal sector. It will serve two purposes: Firstly, the human asset can be profitably absorbed in this sector and secondly, the scarce capital might be released for other purpose due to the labour intensity of this sector.

The reasonable conclusion is to develop both formal and informal sector as a complementary to each other. And if it is possible, it could protect a large number of workers of the informal sector against the period of transition from the existing technology to higher technology. Thus, technological unemployment can be controlled. In fact, if there is a fair trial over the informal sector for boosting up production and additional employment, it is obvious that this sector will emerge as a viable sector and work as good segment of the rest of the economy. Of course, to this end, government assistance is a must.

One of such assistances might be in the form of fresh investment. "The basic consideration in allocating investment... must be to choose each unit of investment that will ultimately give each person.... greater production power than any other alternative".[g] This objective will be satisfied if there is new investment in the informal sector. Because, in a competitive frame work, the productivity of informal sector is not, by any means, less than that of formal sector.[h]

The basic task is of two fold: firstly, to maximize the amount of capital per worker absorbed in the informal sector; and secondly, to upgrade their quality (e.g. skill, energy, perceptiveness, capacity to grip economic opportunities etc.) which will, in turn, expend the entrepreneurial ability. This will be beneficial for the overall economy as the entrepreneurs have the ability to discover new channels of investment and to exploit the basic and available resources most profitably. "The general rule is that nations engaged in reconstruction or development should economies in the use of scarce capital by concentrating on capital light investment".[i] This is also a solicitation to invest in capital light sector of which informal sector is a notable part.

There is another advantage in a prima facie presumption in favour of capital light industry because of its short-lived investment. The inflationary pressure that may be created by new investment will exist for a little time as such a pressure will be balanced as soon as output begins to appear in the market.

To sum up, investment in the informal sector is justified from several points of view. Due to the paucity of capital in the developing country like India, there should be more investment in human capital and not in physical capital.

Thus we come to realize the important role that can be played by the informal sector with context to India. However, this is at best one side of the spectrum. In the other side, we should also consider how this sector, for the sake of its proper functioning, could be ameliorated?

In order to highlight this particular fringe, we have formulated some ameliorative proposals. These are exhibited in the following way:

***Suggestions for Timber and Plywood Industry*[j]**

(1) The existence of middlemen in timber trading should be done away with. Government distribution of machinery should be created and located within the geographical boundary of the areas. Smaller units should be given preference in the matter of allocation of timber. Availability of timber may also be improved.

(2) The problem of shortage of fund may be mitigated through widening the scope of institutional finance. Nationalised banks should help the smaller units with finance to a great extent. The terms of the loan should also be different for different groups of units. Loan on easier terms should be offered to the smaller units. Moreover, the smaller is the unit, the larger is the labour capital ratio i.e. additional employment generation per unit of additional capital would be more in case of a small unit than in case of a large unit.

(3) Problem of shortage of space can be mitigated to a certain extent if drying up of veneers is made with the help of mechanical driers that involve huge capital

investment and it is not possible, therefore, for each unit to afford to have a drier. It costs minimum Rs. 1.5 lacs. It may be suggested that for a number of plywood units, a drier may be installed, with the help of bank finance and under the control of Directorate of Cottage and Small Industries, West Bengal.

Use of drier will increase the cost of production. But, simultaneously, two kinds of saving in respect of cost may be thought of: a) Saving on account of rent to be paid for the land used for drying up of veneers: and b) Saving on account of lowering of prices of timber resulting from the abolition of middlemen in the timber trade. In order to solve the problem of shortage of space created by storing of timber logs, three suggestions can be made:

(i) Creating more vacant space in the locality by way of shifting some Kacha household units and other non-dominant small manufacturing units to some other places.

(ii) Gearing up the inventory control by all the units and

(iii) Reducing fluctuation in the prices of timber.

(4) Problem of lack of machinery may also be solved with the help of bank finance.

(5) There is enough scope of expanding export. The capable units must be helped to procure sophisticated machineries and superior qualities of timber so as to produce exportable qualities of plywood. The exporting agencies, both in private and public sector, should come forward with all kind of possible help to these units.

(6) It is a strange finding that the units situated in the

locality do not manufacture decorative plywood for which there is a very good market in West Bengal, especially in Calcutta. The reason is yet to be explored. These qualities of plywood mostly come from Assam and Mysore. The units of Ultadanga should be urged to take up manufacture of decorative plywood.

Suggestions for Slum Industries Based in Pilkhana

Taking stock of our survey in Pilkhana, we could suggest the following measures for implementing growth of slum industries and for better living conditions in such area:

1. A great majority of the units surveyed complained about lack of adequate financial support as the reason for non-expansion of their business. The commercial banks and other financial institutions should, therefore, examine the credit needs of the units and help them, wherever possible.
2. To guard against any possible difficulty, which may crop up if the units are allowed to expand indiscriminately. It is suggested that in the first instance, only such industries may be encouraged to expand where the prospect of marketability of the produce would not be adversely affected.
3. It is seen that a large number of small units do not maintain even a rough record of such essential information as sales, pending orders, purchases etc., which are regarded as essential prerequisites of eligibility of getting financial assistance from banks. It is, therefore, suggested that once a group of units is identified for financial assistance by the banks, the owners/managers/key men of those units may be suitably trained in the

field of management, accounts and record keeping and other allied aspects to enable them to qualify for grant of institutional finance.

Suggestions for an Overall Development of the Informal Sector

Support of the informal sector appeared to offer the possibility of helping the poor without affecting the rich,- a conciliation between pressures for the redistribution of income and wealth and the desire for stability in favour of economic and political elites. However, it should be kept in mind that whatever might be the government policy towards the informal sector, it must reflect the overall conception of the structure and functioning of the prevailing socio-economic system and the role of state within it.

In order to launch an overall development for the informal sector, which, in effect, trickles down the benefit of development to the marginalized masses, the following suggestions may be prescribed:

1. Subcontracting should be strongly encouraged by the state so that the small units can evolve and incorporate into the national and international economy. In addition, the indigenous entrepreneurs should be encouraged and labour intensive process should be patronized.
2. There should be strict government regulation for abolishing the exploitative link between formal and informal sector. Besides, collectivization of small enterprises with strong state support will be of much help, as it will make enterprises capable of competing more effectively with large firms.

3. There should be the implementation of urban infrastructure construction programmes; this will act as a device for uplifting the level of employment in the urban labour force and retraining of the unemployed for suitable employment. In addition, productive employment opportunities in the informal sector should be promoted and slum clearance activities that destroy the prevailing small-scale activities should be checked. Special measures to provide employment for the educated unemployed can also be solicited.
4. Investment in the informal sector should be enhanced by experiments. Lending procedures should be based on expected production. Besides, the related paper works should be brought to a minimum. In the area of 'formation of human capital', proper policies for developing vocational and managerial skills in the informal sector should be framed.
5. Labour intensive activities should be promoted. A double policy standard should be in operation under which prevailing activities would continue to operate under the old rules while new activities are subject to the changed policies.
6. The government should take necessary measures designed to redirect final demand towards the informal sector. This will create the way of equal distribution of income through the employment promoting impact of the latter. Government purchases of goods and services (specially, the products amenable to a shift from capital - intensive to labour-intensive suppliers) have

sufficient scope for redirection towards the informal sector. This will shift the final private demand and consequently, there will be less capital and import-intensive public demand.

How to Start With?

The necessary precondition for launching development in the informal sector is that the ameliorative project should be based on some definite programmes. The informal units have grown round family trade in most of the cases. Their skills have not yet been cared properly. To counter with this as well as to make any ameliorative project more effective, the following programmes[(k)] may be considered:

Firstly : Identification of Entrepreneurs

Identification of entrepreneurs is not an easy task. An entrepreneur identified by virtue of skill alone, without established credibility, may end up in frustration and failure to achieve the goal. Experiences show that in small-scale industries sector, entrepreneurs have often failed to achieve the desired goals not so much for lack of skill but mainly for not having means to provide security against the assistance from the financial institution and managerial capabilities. Such failures are not mainly detrimental to the future activities of the entrepreneurs themselves but also force the financial institutions to be more selective in future. Although potential entrepreneurs in the city area will be required to face lesser problems than their counterparts in the backward areas in the district. It has generally been accepted that effective development of entrepreneurship which determines the pace of economic growth in a society, needs organized institutional training at the initial stages followed by counseling services as and when required.

Secondly : Development

In order to implement any development project in favour of the informal sector, it is necessary to develop the human resources belong to this sector; specially, those who have some entrepreneurial potential. Essentially, such a project would create local capabilities for entrepreneurship amongst the socially and economically backward communities and would thus, lay a strong foundation for faster area development.

The programme of work may include: a) programme planning; b) creating right atmosphere in the communities living in the area; c) involving local experts in enterprise building; d) developing support system in the region; e) identifying the entrepreneurial potential in the bustees and developing it through training and follow-up counselling; f) training a group of trainers in motivation development.

At the end of the programmes, the region wil! have the following trained work-force available: i) A group of trainers in motivation development; ii) A group of experts for counselling and enterprise building; iii) A large group of entrepreneurs trained in enterprise building; iv) A small group of officers of the implementation agency experienced in the implementation of this type of programme.

In the course of the programmes, there will be a series of activities and projects in the region, which will galvanise the entire area and create a new awareness in the local community about industrial and other potential activities. This climate will help in creating direct and indirect employment of the local unemployed youth. It will also help in attracting more young persons to industry and trade possible and profitable in the area.

Thirdly : Management Agency

In order to ameliorate the informal sector as a whole, the necessary development project should be implemented quickly. For this purpose, establishment of a suitable executive agency will be necessary for effective management, supervision and evaluation of these activities and organisation of training facilities for trainees and trainers in collaboration with other training organizations and institutions.

The following are some of the areas of activity that may have to be handled by the agency: i) To identify entrepreneurs and assist them in completing the procedural formalities for receiving institutional finance; ii) To select schemes and prepare details to meet the requirements of the different agencies; iii) To work out details of infrastructural facilities; iv) To train entrepreneurs in matters of accounting, administration etc., for successful operation of their units; v) To co-ordinate and assist the entrepreneurs in marketing their products; vi) To organise short and relevant training courses in different areas of skills and simple management methods according to identified needs of the group; vii) To provide technical assistance in matters relating to design, materials testing and quality control with assistance from neighbouring institutes and laboratories.

The executive agency will have to handle the various schemes during implementation and to provide the subsequent post-natal care for the successful operation of these units.

Conclusion

To sum up, unemployed or low-earners should not be

considered in isolation. It is rather prudent to see them in terms of their position within the overall economic structure. Here, the problem lies in the articulation of the capitalist sector and informal sector and the dominative position of the former sector, which ultimately determines the position of the marginalised masses in the urban economy.

However, the following questions should be considered properly before launching any developing project for the informal sector:

Firstly: For what and for whom are development reforms intended ? Are they simply to provide for material wants, or, in addition, to alleviate exploitation, subordination or oppression? If our interest is in growth, then we need to try and understand the process of accumulation and technical changes which lead to the non-intensive utilization of much of the available labour power. On the other hand, if we are primarily interested in welfare the object of the statistical investigation must be the household since this is the primary income sharing mechanism and the operative distinction has to be based on poverty levels or on income levels.

Secondly : whether the increasing interest of policy makers in the informal sector is based on a desire to ameliorate the situation or whether they see the development of the informal sector as actually in their own interest. Is it a matter of simply tolerating this sector or is it functional to the whole capitalist system?

REFERENCES

(a) Schumacher : Unemployment or worklessness (ed.) M. Hoda on "problems of unemployment in India" (Allied publisher : London), p. 74.

(b) Govt. of India : Report of the Committee on Unemployment, New Delhi, February '72, p. 27.

(c) National Council of Applied Economic Research : Techno-Economic Survey, New Delhi, p. 56.

(d) Miyopai Shinopara : Survey of the Japans literature on small industry (ed.) B.F. Hoselitz, Mouton : The role of small industry in the process of economic growth (The Hague, Paris : '68), p. 124.

(e) J. Tinbergen : A case for labour intensive activities in (ed.) M. Hoda, "Problems of Unemployment in India" (Asia Publishing House, New Delhi '74), p. 13.

(f) I.L.O. : Employment Objectives in Economic Development, Geneva, '61, p. 20.

(g) Havery Leibenstain : Economic Backwardness and Economic Growth (John Willey & Sons, MG London & Hopman & Hall, '57), p. 265.

(h) See for example : "Competition between the informal and formal sectors in retailing : The case of Santiago" : Victor. E. Tokman in (ed.) Ray Bromley : "The urban informal sector", pp. 1187-1198.

(i) A.E. Khan on "Investment Criteria" in (ed.) A.N. Agarwala & S.S. Singh : Accelerating Investment in Developing Economies (Oxford University Press, Bombay, '69), p. 131.

(j) This is based on Report no. 48 : June '77 : "A study report on small scale timber and plywood industries at Ultadanga", Economic and Social support programme cell, Director of Planning CMDA.

(k) C.f. Project Report no. 111, July '80 : Socio-Economic Survey in Bustees of Calcutta. CMDA in collaboration with Team Consultant Pvt. Ltd., Calcutta.

Bibliography

Banerjee B., *Women Workers in the Informal Sector of Industry in Calcutta,* p. 68.

Birkbeck C.H., *Vagrant Vultures or Industrial Workers?,* p. 98, 101.

Brahme S. *Producers Cooperative: Experience and Lessons From India,* p. 173.

Breman J. (1976): *A Dualistic Labour System:* a critique of the 'informal sector' concept, p. 16, 21, 158.

Bromley R. (ed): *The Urban Informal Sector,* p. 19, 146.

CMDA. (1977): *Economic and Social Support Programme,* Report No. 47, 48, 111, 112, p. 47, 55, 268, 273.

Economic and Social Survey of Asia and the Pacific (1985): United Nations, p. 169.

Emmerij L., *A New Look at Some Strategies for Increasing Productive Employment in Africa,* p. 246, 247.

Fei J. and Ranis G. (1964): *Development of the Labour Surplus Economy: Theory and Policy,* p. 4.

Gerry C., *Petty Production and Capitalist Production in Dakar: the crisis of self-employed,* p. 151.

Govt. of India: *Report of the Committee on Unemployment,* p. 264.

Hart J. K. (1973): *Informal Income Opportunities and Urban Employment in Ghana,* p. 5, 158.

ILO-ARTEP, *Bangladesh: Selected Issues in Employment and Development,* p. 169, 207.

ILO. *Employment Objectives in Economic Development*, p. 265.

ILO. (1970): *Towards Full Employment: A Programme for Colombia*, p. 7, 8.

ILO. (1972): *Employment, Incomes and Equality: A strategy for Increasing Productive Employment in Kenya*, p. 5, 7, 16, 239.

ILO. (1975): *Calcutta, It's Urban Development and Employment Prospects*, p. 9.

Institute of Social Studies Advisory Service. *The Informal Sector: Concepts, Issues and Policies*, p. 169.

Kalikata Bustee Pragati Sangha (1977): "A Project Report on Small Tanners and Ancillary Groups of Eastern Calcutta," p. 43, 76.

Khan A.E. *Investment Criteria*, p. 267.

King K. (1974): *Kenya's Informal Machine Maker: a study of small scale industry in Kenya's emergent artisan society*, p. 18.

Leibenstain H. *Economic Backwardness and Economic Growth*, p. 266.

Lewis W.A. (1954): *Economic Development With Unlimited Supplies of Labour*, p. 4.

Leys C. Underdevelopment in Kenya: the political economy of neo-colonialism. '64-87, p. 11.

Leys C. Interpreting African Underdevelopment: reflections of the ILO report on employment, incomes and equality in Kenya, p. 11.

Lloyd G.R. *Economic Development With Surplus Labour: some complications*, p. 183.

Marsden. K. *Progressive Technologies For Developing Countries*, p. 247.

Marx, K., *Capital*, p. 120.

Mazumdar D. *The Urban Informal Sector*, p. 13, 21.

Mehta M. *Urban Informal Sector: Concepts, Indian Evidence and Policy Implications*, p. 169.

Moser C. (1977): The Informal Sector or Petty Commodity Production? Autonomy or Dependence in Urban Development, p. 11.

Mukherjee S. *Informal Sector: the Only Hope of the Urban Poor in a Metropolis*, p. 45, 68.

National Council of Applied Economic Research (NCAER) : *Techno-Economic Survey*, New Delhi, p. 265.

Oliveira F. D. *A Economia Brasileira: critica a razao dualista*, p. 20.

Oshima H.T. *Labour Force Explosion and the Labour Intensive Sector in Asian Growth*," p. 176.

Papola, T.S. *Urban Informal Sector in a Developing Economy*, p. 74.

Peattie L.R. (1980): *Anthropological Perspective on the Concepts of Dualism: The informal sector and marginality in developing urban economics*, p. 16.

Sansone D. Technologia Y Empleo En Servicios: el caso del comercio minorista de alimentos en chile, p. 138.

Schumacher. *Unemployment or Worklessness*, p. 264.

Scott J. *Exploitation In Rural Class Relations*, p. 157.

Sethuraman S.V. *The Urban Informal Sector: concept, measurement and policy*, p. 13.

Sethuraman S.V. (ed.): "*The Urban Informal Sector in Developing Countries: employment, poverty and environment*, p. 169.

Sethuraman S.V. *Informal Sector in Indonesia: an assessment of policies*, p. 170.

Shinopara M. *Survey of the Japanese Literature on Small Industry*, p. 265.

Standing G.(1977): *Urban Workers and Patterns of Employment*, p. 21.

Suwatte P. "Informal Sector: concept and appropriate policy, world structural change and it's impact on Asean's employment and manpower," p. 170, 171.

Team Consultants Pvt. Ltd. "Socio-Economic Survey In Bustees of Calcutta." *Report No. 110, 112*, p. 67.

Thomas T.H. and Roychowdhury J.B. (1977): *A Scheme for Resettlement of Small Tanners*, p. 45.

Thorbecke E. "The Employment Problem: a critical evaluation of four comprehensive country reports in ILO, strategy for employment promotion", p. 9.

Tinbergen J. *A Case For Labour Intensive Activities*, p. 265.

Tokman V.E. *Competition Between the Informal and Formal Sectors in Retailing: The Case of Santiago*, p. 137, 138, 143, 266.

Tokman V.E. *An Exploration into the Nature of Informal-Formal Sector Relationship*, p. 175, 176.

Weeks J. (1975): *Policies For Expanding Employment in The Informal Urban Sector of Developing Economies*, p. 5, 182, 203, 206.

Weeks J. and Stewart F. *The Employment Effects of Wage Changes in Poor Countries*, p. 196.

Wright E.O. *Class Boundaries in Advanced Capitalist Societies*, p. 98.

Index

A

Abidjan, 8
Africa, 3
Ahmedabad, 73
Apparel Export Promotion Council, 27
Artisan Community, 54
Assam, 55, 213

B

Bagbazar, 93
Bangalore, 27
Bangkok, 150, 152
Bangladesh, 151
Bank Finance, 47
Bank of Baroda, 37
Bantala, 87, 89,92, 93, 97, 106, 108, 112, 174-176
Bantala Dumping Ground, 101, 103, 108, 111, 113, 114, 174, 179, 183
Barabazar Traders, 53
Behala, 93
Bengal, 41
Bhagavati Committee, 208
Bihar, 38, 55, 139
Bio-Gas Plant, 175, 176
Bombay, 27, 32
Burn Standard Company, 114, 175, 176

C

Calcutta, 17, 24, 26, 27, 31, 32, 38, 40-42, 48, 56, 57, 59, 60, 74, 76, 78-81, 89-93, 101, 103, 106, 128-130, 133, 143, 152, 176, 213
  Industrial Belt, 87
  Industrial Zone, 97
  Informal Sector, 61
  Municipal Corporation, 38
  Port, 31
  Slums, 61
Capitalism, 114, 119
Capitalist, 4
Capitalist System, 133
Chetla Haat, 31
CITU, 35
Clay Modelers Community, 45, 51, 53
Clay Modeling Operation, 55

CMC (Calcutta Municipal Corporation), 87, 88, 90-94, 101, 102 , 114, 175-177, 182
CMDA, 37, 48, 56, 60, 76, 77
CMERI, Durgapur, 176, 183
College and SSI, D/O, 212
Colombia Mission, 5, 6
Communication System, 198
Compost Plant, 179
Conservancy, D/O, 87
Cossipore, 93
Cottage and Small Scale, D/O, 24
Customer's Choice, 168

D

Dacca Muslin, 27
Dadandars, (Specialized Merchants), 39
Dakhin Dara, 106
Delhi, 27, 32
Developing Countries, 118, 137, 148-150, 152, 153, 156, 188, 191, 194, 196, 198-202, 204, 207, 209, 211
Developing Economics, 1
Development Reforms, 219
Dhapa Dumping Grounds, 91, 92
Doll Making, 49, 51-53
  Material Used, 52
Dumping Ground, 101, 110, 114, 175
  Calcutta, 91
Durga Images, 54
Durga Season, 53, 54
Durga-Kali-Jagaddhatri, 53

E

East Pakistan, 26
Economic System, 108
Economy, 6, 123, 126, 133, 145, 152, 154-157, 170, 191, 207, 209, 214
  Industrial, 175
  Underdeveloped, 206
  Urban, 2, 3, 7-9, 138
Education, 6, 7
Education and Training System, 191, 201, 203, 204
Educational
  System, 191, 204
  Policy, 207
Employment, 2, 4-8, 24, 38, 40, 49, 70, 89, 131, 132, 136, 137, 138, 144, 148, 150, 159, 164, 165, 169, 182, 188-190, 191, 196, 199, 200, 202, 204, 206-209, 211, 215
  Problem, 4, 5
  Structure, 30
  Urban, 3, 4
Entally, 38
ESCAP Region, 152

F

Factories Act, 24, 25
Formal School System, 14

G

GADI, 94
Garden Reach, 26-29, 32, 34, 36, 37, 56, 93
Gluing Chemicals, 47
GUL, 103

H

Hari Shah Haat, 31
Howrah, 26, 138, 139, 143
Howrah Haat, 34

I

ILO (International Labor Organization), 1-9, 14, 16, 20, 35, 56, 169, 209
  Country Reports, 8, 9
  Employment Policy, 5
  World Development Program Committee, 189
Immigrants, 139
Immigration, 38, 69
Import Liberalization, 201
Incentives, 197
Indian Legislation, 24
Indian Standard Institute, 42, 45
Individualism, 128
Industrial Groups, 60
Industrial Structures, 207
Industrialization, 149, 166
Industries, 24, 48, 56, 62, 67, 75, 80, 103, 138, 192, 211
  Biri, 61
  Calcutta's Informal Sector, 26
  Clay Modeling, 49, 54
  Clothing, 26, 29
  Electrical, 60
  Engineering, 26
  Garment Making, 38
  Hosiery, 57, 60
  Household, 25
  Informal Sector, 27
  Informal Sector, 61
  Jute, 139
  Large Scale, 192
  Leather-, 38
  Major Informal, 24
  Plastics, 40, 41
  Slum Based, 213
  Slum, 59, 60
  Small Scale, 24, 65
  Tailoring, 26, 27, 32
  Tea, 43
  Timber and Plywood, 41, 211
Industry, 28, 29, 34, 36, 38, 40
  Informal Sector, 40
    Characteristics, 14-15
      Groups, 15-16
Informal Sector
  Industrial Units, 62, 40, 41, 118, 127
  Workers, 41
Institute of Development Studies, 3
Italy, 55

J

Jadavpur, 93
Jakarta, 8
Job Security, 65
Joydev, 109

K

Kadapara and Dhapa, 92
Kali, 53
Karl Marx, 110
Kenya, 3, 9, 14, 189-191
Kenya Employment Report, 190
Kenya Mission, 5, 6, 8
  Report, 189, 190, 191
Krishan Nagar and Santipur (Nadia), 49
Kumartuli, 49, 51, 53, 56
  Artisan Community, 55
  Doll Makers Group, 55
  Image Makers, 55

L

Labour, 3, 45-51, 71, 74, 78, 81, 86, 94, 118, 119, 126, 133, 134, 140, 155, 157, 170, 190, 194, 195, 197, 198, 206, 209, 214, 219
  Intensive Techniques, 195

Relations, 29
Migrated, 144
Urban, 150
Lakshmi, 53
Land Reforms, 6, 8
Lending Procedures, 215
Limuru (Kenya), 189
Lucknow, 26

M

Madras, 27, 32
Maniktala and Barabazar, 53
Market (s), 119, 120, 122, 124, 125, 154, 159, 169, 176, 177, 209, 210, 213
Bagri, 41
Calcutta, 55, 74
Capital, 127
Labour, 2, 7, 126, 137, 138, 142, 149
LDC Labour, 19
Megha and Gopal, 111
METIABRUZ, 26, 27, 36
Migration, 6
Minimum Wages Legislation, 41
Moistalla, 35, 36
Multinational Corporations, 61
Multi-Service Agency, 37
Municipal Act, 185
Muraripukur, 57
Muslims, 70
Mysore, 213

N

Nandy Bagan, 138, 140, 141, 143
Nawab Wazed Ali, 26
Nepal, 55
North Bengal, 48

O

Organized Sector Factories, 40
Orissa, 139
Orissa and Bihar, 69
Ostagars, 28-32, 36, 37, 38

P

Phoolbagan, 38
Pilkhana, 62, 66, 68, 69, 74, 76, 77, 138, 141, 213
Industry, 68
Informal Sector, 77
Slum Industries, 68
Slum, 59, 61, 62
Small Scale Units, 78
Small Scale Industries in-, 80
Pilot Employment Mission, 189
Planning and Polices, 188
Policy of Industrialization, 148
Public Transport Facility, 124
Rural Workers, 6

S

Salt Lake, 92
Samsur Ali, 106-108, 112
Santi Committee, 111
Sao-Paolo, 8
Saraswati, 54
Saraswati Images, 54
Satya Lod, 108
Sector, 216
Agriculture, 8, 129, 150, 166, 169, 176
Capitalist, 131, 132, 134
Formal, 11, 15, 20, 120, 122-127, 130, 141-144, 152, 157, 160, 191, 214
Industrial, 87, 90, 176
Informal, 2-20, 11, 14, 15, 17,

20, 24, 25, 34, 35, 38, 40, 62, 65-67, 78, 81, 85, 119, 120, 125, 126, 128, 130, 132-135, 137-139, 141-145, 148-154, 156-160, 162, 164-167, 169, 170, 188-193, 195, 196, 199, 203, 206-208, 210, 214-216, 218, 219
Large Scale Production, 88
Manufacturing, 10
Modern Capitalist, 2
Modern Industrial, 207
Petty Commodity Production, 86
Private, 15, 134
Self Employed, 3
Small Scale Industries, 216
Unremunerated, 3
Urban Traditional, 3, 86
Sectors of Economy, 200
Shobha Bazar, 57
Small Scale Industries, 56
Social Development, 144
Social Infrastructure, 149, 153
Social Justice, 5
Socio-Economic Structure, 198
Sri Lankan Mission, 6
State Promotion Policy, 25
Suku, 109

T

Tailoring Industry, 34
Features, 34
Tangra, 94, 106-108
Tangara and Ballygunge, 92
Tangra and Tiljala, 38
Tangra Police Station, 111
Tanneries, 38
Tapsia, 106
Target Groups, 9
Teachers Retraining Program, 203
Technical Change, 167
Technical Information Centres, 198
Technological Change, 123
Technology,
Foreign, 15
Industrial, 192
Thailand, 150
Third World, 85, 86, 142
Countries, 2
Timber Trade, 212
Trade Unions, 11, 35, 128, 129
Trade Union Movement, 118, 128
Traditional Occupations, 138
Transport and Communication, 156

U

UK, 55
Ultadanga, 56
Ultadanga Canal, 41
Undivided Bengal, 26
Unemployment, 5-7, 150, 199, 202, 206-208
Unemployment Problem, 1, 167, 189
United States, 55
Urban Informal Sector, 11
Urbanization Program, 148
Uttar Pradesh, 139

W

Wages and Income Policy, 189, 200
West Bengal, 32, 47, 48, 55, 68, 69, 212, 213
Agro-Industries Cop., 179
Government, 41
Tailors Union, 35
Western Capitalism, 4
World Employment Program (ILO), 1, 2, 4, 5, 7, 8